Dutton & Jennings

The Standard Saga

John T. Gorman

Dutton & Jennings:
the Standard Saga
❖

Dutton & Jennings: The Standard Saga

Library and Archives Canada Cataloging in Publication

Gorman, Jack, 1929-
    Dutton & Jennings : the Standard saga / John T. Gorman.

ISBN 978-1-55059-358-7

    1. Dutton, Mervyn. 2. Jennings, Reg. 3. Standard General Inc.--History.
4. Construction industry--Alberta--History. I. Title. II. Title: Dutton and Jennings.

HD9715.C34S73 2008   338.7'624097123   C2008-907299-5

Detselig Enterprises Ltd.

210 1220 Kensington Rd NW
Calgary, Alberta   T2N 3P5
www.temerondetselig.com
temeron@telusplanet.net
p. 403-283-0900 f. 403-283-6947

We recognize the support of the Government of Canada through the Book Publishing Industry Development Program (BPIDP) for our publishing program.

We also acknowledge the support of the Alberta Foundation for the Arts for our publishing program.
SAN 113-0234
ISBN 978-1-55059-358-7
Printed in Canada

Cover Design by James Dangerous

Table of Contents

Foreword

As the inevitability of World War Two loomed in the dying months of the Great Depression of the 1930s, Canada's road and transportation infrastructure remained primitive and outdated.

Reg Jennings, a disenchanted banker, switched careers in the mid-twenties to join a road building crew in Southern Alberta. Slight of build but quick of mind, Reg saw unlimited opportunities to build up the nation's transportation corridors.

During the early months of the war, Britain and its allies issued requests for a network of airports capable of accommodating the Commonwealth Air Training Plan.

About the same time, Mervyn (Red) Dutton was winding up a hall of fame career as a hockey player and executive who had spent his off season months as a dirt mover with his father's railroad grade building outfit.

Reg and Merv came together in Calgary in the early 1940s on the original Calgary airport construction on the tract of land now known as Renfrew. The two men formed Standard Gravel and Surfacing Company of Canada Limited in 1941 and embarked on a bold odyssey, taking on a variety of construction projects including airports, road building, grading, surfacing, housing development services, product manufacturing, pipelines, drive-in theatres and dam building. At one point Standard Gravel and Surfacing Company of Canada Limited was the mother company for thirty-five separate business enterprises.

The reflections in this book represent the stories as told to the author by the two principals in 1973. They shared their stories in a series of interviews in Calgary at their offices, in their homes, and at their winter homes at Borrego Springs, California.

While the manuscript gathered dust for more than thirty years, Gerry Stotts, P.Eng., worked with a group to preserve the roadbuilding lore of Alberta, both in artifacts and in documented history. He urged that the recollections of Reg and Merv be published. Terry Gale, current Vice-President and General Manager of Standard General Inc, agreed. Roy Jennings, son of the founding partner, John Denholm, Keith Matthews, Arnold Welter and Jim McHendry, former Standard employees, also contributed with valuable insights and factual corrections to the manuscript.

The history reflects the recollections of two construction pioneers who contributed not only to the development of new techniques through on the job innovation, it recalls onsite descriptions of road building, dam construction, commercial development, pipelining, mine development and other initiatives.

Reg Jennings

Merv Dutton

THE GUNS OF WAR THUNDERED in the far away Pacific following Japan's December 7, 1941 sneak attack on Pearl Harbor. Their echoes reverberated all the way to the House of Commons in Ottawa. Conservative opposition members bombarded Liberal Minister of Munitions and Supply C. D Howe with criticism over the absence of air defence on what they described as Canada's vulnerable west coast.

Rarely in its brief history had Canadians experienced fear of the hostilities of battle on their home soil. In foreign wars, Canadians spilled their blood in South Africa, France, Germany and Southeast Asia. Currently Canadian forces and the allies were engaged in hostilities against Hitler and the Nazis of Germany. But the possibility of a Japanese attack on Canada's west coast in early 1942 posed an unthinkable threat, and launched a wave of anxiety across the nation. Canadian troops, along with their Commonwealth allies, were pre-occupied with the war against Hitler's Nazis in Europe.

On June 4, 1942, R. T. Elson, Washington correspondent for the Southam News group of Canadian newspapers wrote:

"Detailed maps seized from Japanese spies disclosed many months ago to army and navy intelligence officers that Alaska was the preferred road by which the Japanese some day counted on invading the Western Hemisphere. These maps indicated the Japanese planned to invade Alaska and press southward to the United States through Canada."

The seed of fear had been planted in the hearts of Canadians. Eighteen days later, a tangible jolt of anxiety gripped the nation from coast to coast. On that date, a Canadian Press story quoted Defence Minister Ralston from Ottawa:

"Two enemy aircraft took part in the Saturday night shelling of the government wireless and telegraph station at Estevan Point on the West Coast of Vancouver Island."

While there was a later debate whether the shelling originated with aircraft or a Japanese submarine, Prime Minister Mackenzie King described the shelling as the first attack on Canadian land since Confederation. "It should bring home to Canadians the nearness and the vastness of the danger," said the Prime Minister.

It did, and it precipitated vituperative attacks against the Liberal government for its lack of preparedness to face a foreign enemy. The Tory opposition launched a verbal flagellation of the Prime Minister, his Defence Minister Ralston and the testy Minister of Munitions and Supply C. D. Howe.

C. D. Howe was blunt, straight-forward and spontaneous in all his dealings, and he abhorred the petty practice of parliamentary bickering and carping. Howe deflected the criticism, and under pressure set out to shore up the vulnerable defences of Canada's West Coast.

He engaged the drama head-on, and was determined to move quickly. He kept a file of key phone numbers handy, and instructed his parliamentary minions to contact a number in Calgary. The call was directed to one of Howe's acquaintances, the equally feisty western contractor Mervyn A. "Red" Dutton.

Dutton had been a soldier, hall of fame hockey player and iron-fisted president of the National Hockey League. Howe knew him well enough to be confident. Dutton and his partner Reg Jennings thrived on big challenges. He had expressed confidence in their growing reputation of big achievements in the construction field.

Dutton and his partner Reg Jennings, with their burgeoning company, Standard Gravel and Surfacing, had performed some remarkable achievements out west building airports for the Commonwealth Air Training Plan. The partners accomplished high grade performance through an unique blend of Dutton's fiery and aggressive style and Jennings' cool, calculating mastery of the techniques of business management.

Howe wanted to show the Canadian people an immediate gesture to restore a feeling of security against a foreign aggressor. He was aware that the vast forests and rock of the northern British Columbia coast was unguarded and vulnerable. His strategy was to build a show of air defence, an easy solution on paper, but in reality the physical challenges were staggering. He wanted an airport capable of launching fighter plane counterattacks, and he wanted it fast.

Defence strategists in Ottawa scoured maps of the coastal regions and selected a site eighty miles south of Prince Rupert at a small siding called Woodcock. It appeared to be an ideal site for an airstrip if such a thing was possible in a remote wilderness. Woodcock was located on a wide, flat valley tucked into a valley of the Skeena River.

Minister Howe's primary enemy was time, or an absence of it. Already late in June, he knew that the rainy season would make construction activity impossible in about eighty days. The heavy, persistent, saturating rains would render dirt moving, construction and asphalting impossible. Neither Dutton nor Jennings had the faintest inkling of Ottawa's strategic planning. They were totally absorbed with the construction demands of wartime. New work was coming at a fast and furious rate for the fledgling Standard Gravel and Construction firm, recently incorporated by the two partners.

Howe's phone call rang through to the Calgary office of Standard, but not surprisingly Dutton was out of town, ramrodding an airport job at Brandon, Manitoba. Reg Jennings fielded the call, and was instructed in terse terms to find Dutton and order him to contact Minister Howe by telephone as quickly as possible.

Dutton recalls the moment vividly. "I called Howe's office, and all he told me was 'I want to see you right now . . . get to Ottawa as fast as you can.'" Dutton said he rushed to the Calgary airport and boarded an airplane that afternoon, arriving at Howe's office the next morning. With a wry smile, he said he knew better than to demand an explanation over the phone.

Howe didn't waste words. A quick hand shake, something that resembled a greeting, followed quickly by: "Red, I want you to go to a place called Woodcock, and I want an airport built there." The minister addressed Dutton as 'Red', the nickname he had earned as a feared and fiery red-headed National Hockey League defenceman. The minister further explained that he was on the carpet for neglecting to have the West Coast defence in order. Red knew it was a condition that was about to be remedied fast, come hell or high water.

"Do you know where Woodcock is?" challenged the minister.

"Hell no," boomed Dutton.

Howe led him to a map. "It's right here between Vanderhoof and Prince Rupert. Now you get the hell up there, look the site over and report back to me how long it will take to build an airport."

The minister's sense of urgency and frankness inspired Dutton's enthusiasm for the project. Whether it could be built was not questioned at all, only how long it would take.

Dutton said he trusted Howe's judgment. He knew the man was no stranger to the construction business. During the 1920s Howe had designed and built most of the major grain ports and elevators along the Great Lakes. During those boom years of international trade, Howe and his engineering and consulting firms were in demand throughout the world.

"I want one strip and I want it here," Howe said pointing a determined finger at a spot on the map.

Red said he wasn't about to let this opportunity pass him by. He decided instantly that his burgeoning construction firm would take on the project. And besides, he was pretty certain that Howe wouldn't take no for an answer anyway.

"We'll build it, but we need some priorities," Dutton responded.

"Priorities for what?" shot back Howe. "Get out there, assess the situation and get back to me." Howe couldn't see the smile on Red's face as he headed out to the door.

Red immediately searched out a phone and relayed the story to Jennings back in Calgary. They agreed that Dutton should proceed directly to Vancouver, where Jennings would arrange to send Herb Laughlin, the company's construction superintendent.

Moments after the rendezvous, the two men were on their way to a naval base at Bella Coola. Red did some persuasive talking, and convinced the navy to fly himself and Laughlin to Prince Rupert, the nearest air strip to the proposed new site at Woodcock.

"But we were still eighty miles away and too damn anxious to do any waiting," said Red. "I told the agent at the railway station that I needed to look at something for the government, and I guess it sounded impressive because the guy took me right over to the section foreman."

Red recalled using the words: "government priority." He convinced the agent it would be out of the question to wait for the next train headed south.

"I told him I had to be in Woodcock by day break, not really expecting the man to come up with a solution. I mean what could he do, there wasn't a train within a couple hundred miles, but I had to at least try."

Dutton's persuasive plea apparently impressed the section foreman, and he quickly offered a solution. He offered to take Red and Laughlin to Woodcock aboard the little motorized 'speeder' with its four steel wheels gauged to ride the railway tracks.

"By now it's dark, and here we are crowded into this thing . . . Herb is in the back and I'm up front with this guy at the controls. It moves like a bullet down the track, and every second it seems like we just miss hitting a moose or a deer."

They arrive unscathed at their destination at about four in the morning. There doesn't appear to be much in the way of activity or development. A small station house with a shanty behind it stood near the tracks.

"I walked over to this place and rapped on the door," Dutton recalled, not knowing who or what might answer. "After what seemed like forever a head appeared, and the guy is obviously a little concerned about what's going on."

Dutton asked the bewildered figure if they had indeed found Woodcock. He remembered thinking at the time it was one hell of a poor site for an airport.

"Yep," came the reply.

Red grinned and recalled thinking that he might just as easily have said he was the front man for a three ring circus, as it wouldn't have prompted a more incredulous look.

"An airport. There's no place you can build an airport here," the man stammered.

Dutton said he understood the man's reluctance to believe such a proposition. Here it was four a.m. deep in the heart of the forested wilderness, and some stranger comes knocking at your door to talk about building an airport.

"But damn it," Red said, "I had ninety days to accomplish precisely that, and every minute is important. I repeated my statement to the man that an airport will be built here and I've got to have some help."

Finally the man from Woodcock, an employee of the railway, agreed to listen. Obviously he believed this stranger in the night was serious. The station man invited Dutton and Laughlin into the cabin for breakfast and some 'man-to-man' talk.

As the sun peeked over the horizon, Dutton gave the section man fifty dollars, thanked him for the speeder ride and wished him Godspeed on the return trip to Prince Rupert. As the man climbed aboard, Dutton advised him it would best serve the interests of the country if nothing was said about the venture. Red and Herb then turned to survey their surroundings, and were momentarily stunned by the reality of what greeted them.

"I looked at the first tree ten yards away and there was nothing but thousands more just like it all the way to the river," said Red. "Solid timber, and we had to clear this stuff and come up with a finished runway."

Laughlin assured him it could be cleared and graded, but the speed of getting the job done would depend on the availability of equipment and manpower. The only available work force was an Indian tribe in a settlement about two miles up the track.

If the Indians would accept the work, thought Red, at least the project could be launched. He set out to meet the chief. The meeting turned out to be productive and Dutton came away with the chief's commitment to provide the clearing crew. He and Laughlin then caught the next train out of there and returned to Calgary and a consultation with Jennings.

Reg wrung the best information he could from the two of them and after a few calculations, confirmed that the job could be done in ninety days.

"I remember asking Merv at the time just how the government was going to pay for it," recalled Reg. "He told me he didn't know for sure but before I could object he added 'but they're sure as hell going to pay for it, you can bet your ass on that.'" Jennings said later he never addressed his partner as Red, always Merv.

The Woodcock job would typify Dutton-Jennings operating procedure. Dutton was the front man, making the contacts, promoting the company's capabilities. Jennings' share of the duties included the estimating, organization, logistics, financing and general administration.

"Dutton didn't know whether we had a dollar or a million dollars, and he didn't seem to give a damn," Reg said, reflecting on the early days of the partnership. But he trusted his partner's judgment and abilities as he despatched Dutton to Ottawa with his blessing and a positive answer for the Woodcock project. He added a firm admonishment that he had better come back with some advance cash to pay for labor, supplies and equipment.

Dutton promised Minister Howe the airstrip could be built in ninety days provided the weather cooperated and some priorities were met. He explained that asphalt was scarce and the government would have to ensure that adequate supplies would be at the Woodcock siding when the grading phase was complete. Apprehensively, he then tackled the issue of price with the minister.

"Prices hell," Howe roared. "Get out there and build that airport and we'll talk prices later."

That was good enough for Dutton. He was confident the compensation would be fair and just, and he felt the minister's compelling urgency to get the project underway.

During subsequent meetings between Howe and the Dutton-Jennings partnership discussions on priorities resurfaced more than once. Dutton and Jennings were in the middle of building airports at Calgary and Brandon, both government contracts, and all of their heavy equipment was tied up on these jobs.

Howe was undeterred. "Well for the defence of Canada you better get out of there and get that goddamned airport finished at Woodcock," he said. "You can come back and finish the other airports later."

Supervisory staff had been dispatched to Woodcock to work with natives on the clearing phase. The next and most urgent hurdle was to organize the mammoth logistics of marshalling equipment and camp facilities to the site. Bulldozers, scrapers, trucks, Letourneau earth movers, a crushing plant, an asphalt plant, paving machines, cement mixers and an entire prefabricated plant were loaded in Calgary on thirty eight freight cars. Jennings organized the company's key personnel for each of the various phases of the project and arranged to move them in and out of Woodcock as they were needed.

The train chugged through Edmonton, across to Prince George and pulled into the Woodcock siding, where the native clearing crew looked on in bewilderment. And that nervous little station master would no longer be lonely at least for ninety days.

The government had provided no specifications and no engineering data for the airstrip project. The lone representative of Howe's department was an instrument man, a former architect who watched in wide eyed amazement as the Dutton-Jennings crew transformed the tranquil, sylvan valley into yet another high intensity industrial venture.

"This guy didn't know much about construction, so I became the engineer on the job," Dutton said.

The area was clear a few feet back from the river, but the swamp shrubs merged with an endless stand of heavy timber. Dutton and the government instrument man made some primitive soil tests and determined the whole valley was a sea of fine silt. Dutton quipped at the time the soil would make one hell of a fine garden, but fell a long distance short of a support base for an airport runway.

Dutton knew there was a solution, but he also saw it as a good opportunity to tease the government man.

"There's no way we can consolidate this stuff, it's solid silt. We can't build an airport on this," said Merv.

The government man, fear springing across his face, danced from one nervous foot to the other and tried to wring the panic from his sweating hands.

"I don't know what we can do," he whimpered. "Maybe I had better phone Ottawa."

It was just the straight line Dutton had hoped for.

"I don't care what the hell you do," Dutton roared. "But while you're on the phone I'll be out here building an airport. We're going into this stuff with our scrapers, and we'll go as deep as necessary to get stability."

The dozers attacked the trees with an unforgiving vengeance. And as they fell to the forest floor, the crew of about thirty Indians had moved them into piles where they were sorted for useable timber and waste.

And then came the scrapers, burrowing deeper and deeper into the silt beds. It was too much for the government man.

"How deep are you going to go?" he asked Dutton.

"I don't know," replied Merv. "You tell me." He wasn't surprised not to get an answer.

At the fourteen-foot depth level, Merv knew he needed some gravel for fill, because it appeared the silt depth would be endless. At the rate they were digging, it would be the world's first underground airport. Fortunately, he found a productive gravel source in the nearby sandbar on the Skeena River.

Trucks were mobilized and hauled gravel to the airstrip site. The entire dimensions of the airport were treated the same — twelve to fourteen feet of overburden were removed until an area 6,000 feet long by a mile wide was stabilized with fourteen feet of high grade gravel.

Now for Dutton the whole thing was a lot of fun. He was in his element, and thrived on accomplishing the project's challenging engineering tasks that seemed to confront him on a daily basis.

But back in Calgary, Reg was getting a touch nervous as Ottawa still hadn't come up with any money. Almost as nervous, in fact, was the company's bank manager, who watched a steady flow of cheques written for relatively huge denominations flow through a barren account.

"That banker was pretty good to us," recalls Reg. "We had always met our commitments, but this time he hadn't seen us for three months and he was getting nervous as hell."

Reg went to his partner with a timely message.

"For Christ's sake, Merv, we've got to get some money out of this outfit (Ottawa) somewhere."

Dutton fired off a telegram to C. D. Howe. "The toilet paper and the buttons are all gone – what do we do now?" was the text of the wire.

As near as Jennings can recall, the government forwarded an advance to Standard's Calgary bank, and the heat was temporarily off.

At about the same time, back in Calgary, Bob Burns – a gentle giant of a man towering well over six feet – was getting involved with Dutton's son, Norman, in the creation of a small concrete contracting company. The share distribution followed the traditional Jennings-Dutton formula of equal partnership in all ventures. With the embryonic Burns and Dutton construction company, it was one-third Dutton, one-third Jennings and one-third Burns.

Burns' arrival on the scene was timely and significant. He was an expert in the handling of concrete, a skill he had learned from his father. Burns got the call from Dutton to drop everything he was doing in Calgary and proceed to Woodcock, where completion of the airport contract required drainage gutters, manholes and storm drains leading back to the river.

He arrived on site with a portable gasoline engine mixer and his formula for success . . . a bag of cement, two workers shoveling in seven times that amount of sand, and another one squirting enough water to make it a soupy mix.

Dutton spent most of the summer ramrodding the Woodcock job. Jennings appeared periodically to supervise the technical preparation for the gravel and surfacing. Reg's capacity for invention and innovation introduced many short cuts to traditional construction methods.

The end of September was drawing near, and the crew knew the deadline would be met.

"We were loading up the equipment, and as we threw the last mattress into the car, it started to sprinkle," Reg said.

Through that final night, the rain increased in intensity and didn't stop for almost a month. The airport was finished, a shimmering expanse of asphalt in the British Columbia wilderness.

"As far as Reg and I know, they never landed an airplane on it," Dutton said. "But we kept our commitment to C. D. Howe, and it sure as hell helped when he was awarding contracts for building the Commonwealth Air Training Plan airstrips all over Western Canada."

A RICKETY, ONE-STOREY FRAME STRUCTURE perched on blocks housed the Union Bank. It was the proudest building on the main street of Foremost, a tawdry little town in the depressed area of south-central Alberta, a few miles north of the U.S. border. Its pale yellow exterior, pallid and flaked, was the bank's contribution to the village's gangly, clapboard architecture. It was 1926.

Winds drifting eastward out of the Crowsnest Pass, accelerating at Pincher Creek, and howling out of control at Lethbridge, had pummeled the buildings of Foremost into rows of uniformly misshapen parallelograms.

Cattle stealing, liquor running, smuggling, illegal entry and the flights of criminals were fringe benefits of life along the 49th parallel, which separates the western prairies of the United States from those of Canada. The Royal Canadian Mounted Police patrols along the border were a moderately successful deterrent to the highly active bank bandits of Montana, who were known to covet quarry in the small towns north of the border in Canada.

The bank at Foremost, thirty miles north of the border, offered an enticing target too rich to resist. During the bank's first few weeks of service, liquid securities and cash were stored in a strong box under a bed where the manager slept.

A venturesome gang of Montana bandits got wind of the arrangement, and planned a night raid on Foremost.

Before their arrival, security had improved. The manager was comfortable in his new home, and the bank had acquired a sturdy safe.

The bed was still there, occupied by two junior clerks, Reg Jennings and Nick McPhee. Under the bed, the manager's dog slept soundly. The bank had two small rooms at the rear. A small hallway separated them from the main business area where the large time-locked safe was housed.

The bandits gained entry through an open window into the room where the clerks were sleeping in the sagging double bed. The manager's dog stirred curiously, crawled out and greeted the intruders with a yawn and a wag of his tail.

"I had a colt automatic revolver under the pillow," Reg recalls. "The first thing the lead bandit did was reach under the pillow and grab the gun."

"What's this doing here?" he growled.

Reg concluded that the gang had done a thorough "casing" job on the bank and its operations and that co-operation and prudence were to be the better part of valor.

Reg and his partner having been awakened rudely and at gunpoint were intimidated into submission. They were instructed to open the safe. Jennings, with a gun in his ribs, complied, and after fumbling nervously with the lock, he eventually twisted the correct combination of numbers, and the outer doors of the vault fell open. McPhee was securely gagged and bound, hands behind his back on the bed.

"They stuck a gun in my ribs and ushered me to the big safe in the main banking room. It was a double door, heavy-duty safe, about six feet high with a cash compartment behind the inside door. They knew I had the combination of the outside door, but they didn't know I had the combination of the inside door," Reg remembers.

Reg Jennings

"With a few convincing jabs of the gun in my ribs, they persuaded me to open the outside door, but they didn't say a damn word about the inside door. Still, with the uncomfortable feel of the cold steel in my ribs, they herded me into the other room and persuaded me to open the two smaller safes — one which contained the bonds and securities, and the bank's ledgers and records."

Reg was taken back to the bedroom, where he was gagged and bound hand and foot. The head bandit, Johnny Reid, alias "Smilin' Johnny Reid", sat on the bed with the two bank clerks while the other members of the gang prepared to blow the main safe.

"God I was really scared then," Reg recalls. "I wasn't frightened when they first came in — but it was a peculiar feeling — when I knew they were going to blow that safe. I thought my God, they'll blow half this building away."

The bandits placed a mattress on the floor in front of the safe, and proceeded to blow the heavy door off its hinges. The robbers eventually made off into the night with about $12,000 in cash, a bag full of securities, and headed south across the border.

Ironically, the Alberta Provincial Police detachment was right across the street from the bank, and the policeman sleeping in the building snoozed peacefully through the explosion undisturbed.

Jennings and McPhee, working together in a frustrating blind fumble, eventually unbound each other and galloped across the street to rouse the sleeping policeman.

"He was more excited than we were," said Reg.

"What in hell should we do?" said the animated policeman.

He calmed down long enough to decide his first move would be to telegraph the Lethbridge detachment. The trio rushed to the railway depot to discover the telegraph wires leading from the station neatly cut and dangling in the soft morning breeze. Doubling back, they headed for the telephone office on the dead run, where they found more slashed cables hanging against the side of the building. They knew now they were dealing with experts.

The RCMP officer then armed Jennings and McPhee with high-powered rifles and ordered them back to the bank to stand guard. The policeman then sped off to Bow Island, thirty miles north, seeking help.

"I'll always remember McPhee and me sitting on that bed with these big goddamn rifles – guarding the barn long after the horse is gone," Reg said.

Eventually the policeman returned with a battalion of police officers and Pinkerton agents.

"They asked us hundreds of questions, but it eventually turned out to be one big party. These cops congregated in the bank every night for about a week. Some searched around looking for leads, but most of them sat around drinking booze and telling stories," Reg said. "It was during prohibition, and they had large stocks of booze confiscated. It was one big party for about a week."

The bank robbers eventually ran out of cash, and about a year later, Jimmy Wilson tried to cash some of the stolen securities with a bootlegger named "Daddy" Marshall in

Havre, Montana. When the bootlegger took the bonds to the bank, the case was quickly solved and the bandits were all rounded up in the Havre district.

The robbery and a number of other minor irritations eventually drove Reg and Nick out of the banking business and into separate and highly successful careers. McPhee eventually became the president of Sick's Breweries. Ironically, one of the bandits, years later, wound up as a salesman for the brewery in Great Falls, Montana.

"I got completely fed up with this damn banking business — mind you, it was a great experience," Jennings recalls. "I walked into the manager's office and I said, 'Mr. Hunter, I'm leaving.'

"'When are you leaving?' he asked.

"'Tomorrow morning,' I said.

"And then he raised hell in general and threatened that I wouldn't get my pension contribution and other savings unless I gave thirty days notice. I told him it didn't make much difference to me, I was going anyway."

For the next several months, Reg performed odd jobs around Foremost, until September 1926, when his life was to take a dramatic turn.

"I heard about an outfit that was just starting to gravel the roads from Coutts, on the U.S. border to Lethbridge. I went down to see Jay McLaughlin, a road builder and construction man from Great Falls, Montana, and his partner, a rough-hewn Swede named Albert Carlson. The contract called for gravelling the road from Coutts to Warner immediately, and from Warner to Lethbridge the following year.

"I could sure use you," McLaughlin said to Reg, "but I can't pay you because we haven't got any money."

"You can give me room and board," Reg insisted.

McLaughlin agreed.

"And that's how I started working with Jay McLaughlin." McLaughlin eventually became one of the major project contractors in the United States northwest.

Reg became enthralled immediately with the road surfacing business, and flew at his new duties with enthusiasm. The work consisted of keeping time and other odd jobs, but Reg had an intuition very early that his skills and organizational capabilities would adapt easily and quickly to the road building business.

McLaughlin grew very fond of Reg. He was particularly indebted to him for his deft handling of Carlson, who in a fit of drunken temper, would periodically assault McLaughlin.

"The old Swede would get mad, then he'd get drunk, and then he'd take after McLaughlin with whatever was lying around – a two by four, a pick handle or whatever. I would always intervene, and one way or another settle him down. I would offer him a beer, and then reason with him on the futility of violence."

The work progressed well that fall, with ideal weather in October and November. McLaughlin returned home to Great Falls and asked Reg to stay on with Carlson during the winter to look after the horses and equipment.

Most of the motive power for the heavy equipment was supplied by horses. The company owned a small gravel-crushing plant, which was powered by a caterpillar tractor.

Reg occupied himself, buying hay, feeding the horses, and repairing the equipment. He and an engineer on the crew overhauled the caterpillar, replacing a lot of worn parts. It was in prime condition to begin work in the spring.

McLaughlin had left about $12,000 in the bank at Warner to cover expenses for the winter operation.

"I was buying hay groceries and machine parts and Carlson was signing the cheques," Reg said. "It turned out he signed a lot of cheques – in fact, he was spending money like a drunken sailor, a lot of it on booze. Anyway we ran out of money, and I told Carlson we'd better do something if we were going to keep the outfit together.

"'We'll have to phone Yay,' he said.

"We phoned 'Yay' alright, and did he raise hell."

McLaughlin returned to Warner in a surly mood, but determined to work things out. He was growling when he arrived. "Now we're in a helluva fine pickle," said McLaughlin. "Here we are about to start up for spring and we're broke."

Reg accompanied McLaughlin to the bank in Warner, where they arranged for a $3,000 loan. It was enough to finance the spring start-up.

"Spring broke beautifully that year. It was 1927," Reg recalled. "The weather was ideal, the equipment performed beautifully, we got a lot of work done and we made damn good money."

When that job was finished, McLaughlin and Carlson moved on to Edmonton to bid on widening and gravelling the road from Airdrie to Red Deer. Their bid was unsuccessful, and it was awarded to a man named Belyea, a crude and crusty entrepreneur who operated the Commercial Cartage Company in Calgary.

Belyea didn't have any equipment, so he came to Warner and made a deal to buy McLaughlin and Carlson's outfit.

"It wasn't a cash deal, so it was arranged that I would follow the equipment to protect McLaughlin's interest," Reg recalled.

Everything, including horses, dirt moving equipment, gravel crusher and tractor was moved from Warner to Beddington, just north of Calgary. There was a small railroad siding there, and it was conveniently located near a gravel pit.

"We crushed gravel there all that year and shipped it in railway cars right to Red Deer, where it was unloaded and hauled down the highway. At the time, I was working for both Commercial Cartage and Carlson, as an odd jobber and time keeper," Reg recalled.

It turned out that Carlson and Belyea were two of a kind, and the booze flowed endlessly. Jennings not only anchored the business end of the arrangement, he played the role of peace maker when the two revelers disagreed.

The job was finished later in the fall of 1927, and the outfit was moved to Cardston, where it was employed gravelling the road from Cardston to Waterton Lakes. When the surfacing work on the Waterton highway was completed in 1928, the Commercial Cartage outfit moved back to Calgary.

Reg had become a keen student of gravel and surfacing techniques, and in the wake of the storms created by the roistering Belyea, was pretty much left to his own devices to run the operation.

"One of the first big jobs I was on, in the city, was the excavation of Eaton's downtown store basement in 1928," Reg remembers. "That was one hell of a job."

The first gasoline-powered excavating shovel in Western Canada was employed on the Eaton's job. It was owned by Ed Jefferies, who eventually established a thriving construction business in Calgary. Jefferies rented the shovel to Commercial, which owned two wheezing trucks. Fill from the basement was loaded into the trucks and driven out in the country to be dumped. In addition, Commercial supplied sand and gravel from a pit in the Bow River, near the Eau Claire sawmill. It is now Prince's Island.

"We supplied material to damn near every contractor in Calgary," Reg remembers. "That summer of 1928, I didn't get any sleep at all, running from job to job, making sure everything was running smoothly."

Reg caught the odd nap in his Model T Ford pick-up, but he was unflagging in his determination that every job had enough gravel to keep the men and equipment occupied.

With Reg at the helm, Commercial Cartage was given a portion of the work on the Ghost River Dam project, forty miles west of Calgary, where the Ghost River flows into the Bow.

Carlson had been sent off to Canmore on a gravel haul, and he continued his profligate ways and his complete absence of respect for the value of money.

In 1931, Commercial Cartage entered into a joint venture with General Construction of Vancouver on a project to pave the highway from Calgary to Cochrane. It was the first pavement laid in Alberta, and it was to be the first leg of the original Calgary–Banff highway.

Also in 1931, the contract for Calgary's Glenmore Dam was awarded to the pioneer firm, Bennett and White Construction.

Jennings' Commercial Cartage outfit supplied all the materials and performed the excavation work. Again, Reg assumed the role of the peacemaker. His skills in diplomacy were to become an essential factor in his later successes.

Bennett and White brought in an engineering expert from San Francisco named Hindmarsh. Earl Gammon, who later became a prominent federal Conservative party supporter, and a life-long friend of a Saskatchewan lawyer named John Diefenbaker, was also involved in the contract, and he despised Hindmarsh. Earl, who also owned one of Banff's major motels, would periodically imbibe to excess and vent his displeasure on the equally volatile Hindmarsh.

"I was always the guy that had to settle them down before they destroyed each other," Reg remembers.

In 1932, the economy began to deteriorate badly. The Depression was a reality, with no upturn in sight. Construction jobs were scarce in an era when the hard times created shortages of money for both business and government. Belyea persisted in his carefree behavior, and soon his Commercial Cartage Company was bankrupt.

The company operated out of a little office in Riverside, near the Bow River in downtown Calgary. Commercial had occupied a large barn where all the horses, dump wagons and other equipment were housed.

The Trust and Guaranty Company, under the direction of H. J. Howard, was the liquidator. A corporation was formed on behalf of the creditors, and Howard arranged to put Jennings in charge. It was given the name Belyea Construction Limited. That arrangement survived through 1932 and 1933.

"You just couldn't keep track of the fellow Belyea. All he thought about was the money we were taking in – no thought about what had to be paid out," Reg recalls.

"I finally said I can't take any more of this, and in 1934, we called all the creditors together to make a further analysis of the whole thing. Lawyer Eric Harvie acted on behalf of the creditors, and I worked for him while we got it sorted out," Reg said.

It developed that the Belyea construction operation was beyond help. After every potential avenue of re-organization had been pursued, the meticulous Eric Harvie concluded that liquidation was the only remaining choice. It was the end of the line for the construction company, and Reg was out of a job.

It was the low point of the Depression, and job prospects were bleak.

"Things were tough," Reg recalls. "We were turning handsprings for donuts – anything to make a buck."

It turned out that an acquaintance of Reg's, pioneer heavy equipment dealer Harry Oliver, had a contract to operate a water pumping system in Turner Valley. Harry gave Reg the job of operating the pump station in 1935, where he remained until part way through 1936.

Oliver was apparently impressed with Reg's skills and enthusiastic performance. In 1936, well aware of Jennings' achievements in the Belyea operation in spite of the adverse conditions, Oliver suggested Reg return to the gravel and surfacing business, because there were some opportunities beginning to appear. Reg contacted his friend Jay McLaughlin, and arranged for Oliver to buy a gravel-crushing plant and other equipment.

In 1936, with Reg at the helm, Oliver's newly-established construction operation obtained a contract to gravel the road from Waterton Lakes to Fort MacLeod. It was the first time that stretch of road had ever been graveled.

In 1937, as a salaried employee, Reg moved the operation to the original Calgary airport in an area of the city which is now known as Renfrew. It was a sub-contract arrangement with a firm known as Dutton Brothers. Neither Reg Jennings nor Merv Dutton could know their first meeting would become an historic moment in the annals of the Canadian construction industry.

Jennings was everywhere, supervising, analyzing, cajoling and maintaining a strict vigil on the time sheets. He was meticulous about maintenance and operating procedures, and he was becoming a keen student of the techniques of gravel – its origins, its qualities, methods of handling, crushing and surfacing.

The outfit was running at peak efficiency in 1938 when Harry Oliver died. The Oliver estate was practically broke.

Again H. J. Howard of the Trust and Guaranty Company operated Oliver's estate as executor. Howard had no difficulty in assigning Reg to carry on with the gravel and surfacing operation. With the trust company as operator and Reg as general manager, the outfit performed several successful contracts and was well in the black.

"Howard was always good to me, and as the outfit made money, Howard paid me a share of the profits as a bonus," Reg said. "One day, he came to me and said: 'Reg – we've got no damn business as a trust company being in the gravel business – you'd better buy this outfit.'"

"What the hell am I going to use for money?" I asked him.

It turned out Howard was prepared to allocate some of the accumulating profits to Reg, which he added to his modest personal assets, and a purchase arrangement was reached.

It was a pretty heady time for Jennings. Always self-effacing, quick to count his blessings, Reg reflected on his arrival in Canada from England in 1910 as a most fortunate twist of fate.

His father, a barber by trade, settled in Yellow Grass, Saskatchewan. It was one of hundreds of prairie settlements that sprung up along the rail lines as trading centres, and gathering points for the marketing of wheat.

Jennings senior bought a two storey building on the main street. It contained a barber shop and a pool hall, and an upstairs apartment where the family lived. Reg had gone to school in England for about a year, and resumed his studies in the public school at Yellow Grass.

In the dead of winter 1915, a couple of escaped German war prisoners happened through Yellow Grass. For reasons Reg could never understand, they set fire to the Jennings wooden structure and burned it to the ground. The Jennings family was literally homeless, with nothing more than the clothes on their backs in the ten below zero Saskatchewan winter.

Reg's dad built a new house and rented a building in which to carry on his business, but somehow the enthusiasm for Yellow Grass had waned. The family moved to Langham,

Matt Booth on old time grader, 1941

Saskatchewan near Saskatoon, where Jennings senior once again established a barber shop and pool parlor. But he had acquired a wanderlust, and soon he packed up the family and moved to Eckville on the north end of Sylvan Lake in Central Alberta. From Eckville they moved to Bow Island, and from Bow Island back to Eckville, where he tried farming. About 1917, he moved the family once again to Foremost, south of Lethbridge, where he remained in the barbering and pool hall business until his death in 1936.

Reg enjoyed life as a boy in the Western prairie towns. He enjoyed school, even though he moved around a lot. He was also keen to seize opportunities to earn extra money. He was a pin setter in the bowling alley where he earned a nickel a game, and eventually he established a shoe-shine stand in the pool hall. Reg worked his various money-making schemes in the evenings and Saturdays and maintained a good scholastic record during the week. In December 1919, he joined the Union Bank in Foremost as a full time clerk, and began his business career in earnest. It was ironic that the Union Bank was eventually merged with what is now the Toronto-Dominion Bank. Many years later, Reg became a prominent member of the Toronto-Dominion board of directors.

Dutton & Jennings:
the Standard Saga

❖

MERVYN A. "RED" DUTTON lived a bold, larger than life existence in a highly charged atmosphere of excitement and adventure. In contrast to Reg Jennings, his more reserved and cerebral business partner, Dutton's personality exuded an intoxicating energy. An encounter with "Red" Dutton, whether a confrontation or a celebration, would invariably become a stimulating experience.

As a boy Dutton was a gifted athlete, playing hockey, basketball and football in his native Winnipeg. As a teenager, he joined the Canadian army and was severely wounded at the Battle of Vimy Ridge. After a long and painful convalescence, he returned to hockey and became one of the game's greatest stars.

Red managed the old New York Americans, during the 1930s, and became president of the National Hockey League in 1942. And while all this was going on, he maintained an active interest in construction and road building, along with his partner Reg Jennings back in Calgary.

Dutton's crusty exterior could be intimidating at first, but underneath resided a thoughtful intelligence and sense of fair play. His determined, aggressive manner was a perfect complement to the more introspective and retiring personality of Jennings.

Jennings approached business in an academic, almost scientific fashion. His conclusions on techniques, personnel and financial matters were nearly always right. When Jennings reached a conclusion, Dutton backed it and threw his lusty determination behind it. If Jennings had ever been wrong, Dutton could at least attempt to make it right with the force of his personality.

W. A. Dutton was operating a horse-powered railroad construction outfit out of Russell, Manitoba, when his son, Mervyn A. (Red) Dutton was born in 1897. Red's earliest recollections are of horses and men labouring on construction jobs from dawn until dusk. Equally vivid in his memory are a pair of spring skates — a blade attached to his walking boot with a spring at the toe and heel. Merv used them to glide about on a neighbourhood pond at age three.

Sports have been as much a part of Dutton's life as construction and business. His secret in life was the ability to use one to promote the other. Dutton senior was fond of sports and showed his support in a substantial way, sponsoring baseball and hockey teams in several towns including Kenora and Portage La Prairie.

"He always bought me whatever I wanted in the way of sports equipment – skates, sticks, baseball gloves, lacrosse sticks," Red recalls. "When I was seven and eight years old, we skated and played hockey all day long, all winter on the frozen Assiniboine River. Hell, in those days, I ate my meals on skates."

When the Duttons moved to Winnipeg in 1904, they settled near the corner of Ferbie and Cornwall, west of the Assiniboine bridge. Conveniently, the Ryan rink was nearby.

"There was no such thing as organized teams," Red remembers. "About seven or eight of us would get together and challenge the kids playing on the Portage and Broadway rinks."

Modern minor hockey was a disappointment to Dutton, who gave a large part of his life to the sport. It was opinion that too much militancy and organization among kids in the six to twelve age range is ruining Canadian hockey.

"It takes all the fun out of it for them." Red's conviction was: "If you want to get hockey going again in this country, build a rink on every corner where 100 kids can chase fifty pucks."

When he was twelve years old, Dutton took a job with a CPR survey party as a 'get me'. "The men would say, 'get me this or get me that' and it kept me busy all summer."

By this time, Red was enrolled in St. John's College, an Anglican residential school in Winnipeg. It was there he came under one of the important influences of his life, Headmaster Walter Beeman.

"He was one-quarter Metis," Red recalls, "and one of the finest people I have ever met. He liked me, and encouraged me in every way – in athletics and in school work. Walter was a good athlete himself, and if there was a football to be blown up, ice to clean, I was picked to do it."

Dutton's respect for the headmaster has lingered fondly in his memory for a lifetime.

"I was pretty aggressive. When I became unruly, and began to assert myself, Walter took it out of me."

Part of Dutton's fondness for the headmaster relates to à period in his life which he remembers as one of the most exciting. As a rangy, freckle-faced redhead at age fourteen, Red was beginning to attract a lot of attention around Winnipeg for his talent as a hockey player.

Members of the St. John's senior team, playing in a regular league with the University of Manitoba and Wellesley College, wanted to recruit Dutton. Walter Beeman was against it, on the grounds he might learn some bad habits from the older boys. Walter finally submitted to the pressure, and Dutton played senior hockey about three times a week. The headmaster maintained a moral vigil on his protégé, ensuring that he bed down by nine, and that any risk of corruptive influence by the seniors was minimized. He escorted him to the rink, and he brought him home to the college after each game.

"They cleared the way for me to play, and I remember it as the greatest thrill of my life. I didn't sleep the night before that first game. In my mind, I was playing hockey all night – and then the next morning, walking into that Winnipeg auditorium . . . I'll never forget it."

As a teenager, Dutton established himself as a skilled, all-around athlete. He participated with an unyielding enthusiasm in hockey, football and baseball.

Meanwhile, the guns of war were rumbling in Europe. In February 1916, when he was eligible, Red joined the university company of the Princess Pats and trained in Montreal. He journeyed to France as an infantryman, and spent two years less one day on the front line.

He was assigned to a support troop carrying ammunition during the intense battle of Vimy Ridge, when a high percussion shell wiped out seven of his companions.

"All hell broke loose," Red recalls, "and by the time I had realized what happened, chunks of shrapnel had torn away half of my left hip."

Relating the story as a robust eighty-four year old, Red dropped his trousers to half-mast and showed the sixty-five year old scars from his war wounds. It was as if someone had hacked away about one-third of the meaty portion of the upper thigh.

At the time, casualties were so heavy, he lay on a stretcher in a makeshift field hospital five days before the first dressings were applied. The weather was leaden with sleet and snow, as the harried medical workers faced an endless stream of stretcher cases.

Dutton was eventually moved to a hospital near the coast of France, where doctors seriously considered removing his leg above the knee.

"To hell with that," I said. "I could move, and I could make the little cords in my foot move." It was an amazing illustration of the Dutton determination, even though his leg was wracked with gangrene.

A compromise was reached, as the doctors removed twenty-six pieces of shrapnel and, in Red's words, "An amount of flesh equivalent to a ten-pound roast."

During his hospital stay in France, the Germans flew over with Zeppelin balloons and bombed the hospital. The patients were evacuated and Red ended up in a convalescent hospital in Leicester, England. He remained there for seven months, until he eventually arrived at Epsom County Hospital.

"It was a great place — I had the most carefree time I've ever had in my life there," Red recalls.

The experiences with the leg injury illustrate one of the most prominent of the Merv Dutton characteristics — his unflagging determination. While Red was admonished by the medical staff to stay off the leg, he convinced himself that exercise and work would return it to normal strength.

He became a curiosity at Epsom. The only Canadian in the hospital, his boyish features, red hair, freckles and boundless enthusiasm made him a favorite with the nurses.

"I had a great time. I knew the leg was getting better, and I spent most of my time trying to get on the good side of the nurses." He remembers one exceedingly attractive one, who ironically turned out to be his brother's wife's sister.

The dressing was changed every two hours, and the open wound was bathed in a saline solution. Red was allowed to push the 'goodie' cart through the wards, bringing hot chocolate, tea and wine to the wounded soldiers.

The battle in Europe was becoming more intense and eventually, more wounded Canadians arrived at Epsom.

Red continued to work on the leg, even though he was confined to a wheel chair. He wheeled himself about two miles from the hospital to a roller skating rink every day. There, he would roller skate three or four hours. Later he did a lot of hiking, and eventually conditioned the leg to the point it was stronger than the other.

He suffered one minor setback near the end of the convalescent period. He was moved to a camp near Epsom Downs, where there was a large contingent of Canadians. One day, a baseball game was organized, and characteristically, Dutton was one of the prominent competitors. In his enthusiasm, he ripped open the leg wound sliding into second base. It became infected, and set his convalescence back several weeks. As he grew into middle age and later, Red claimed he could predict a weather change two days in advance because of the wound.

Dutton was discharged in 1919 and was awarded a six dollar per month disability pension because, in addition to the leg wound, he suffered a broken ear drum at Vimy Ridge.

The war ended with the German surrender in November 1918. With his army career behind him, Dutton began taking a serious look at the future. In keeping with his bold outlook on life, he launched an adventurous and expansive lifestyle pattern that he would cultivate for the rest of his life. The principle ingredients were sports, construction and hard work.

On the construction segment, he began working for his father, who was primarily a railroad roadbed contractor. Red learned the rudiments of construction bookkeeping and timekeeping, and in the early going spent a lot of time feeding, watering and harnessing the horses which provided the power for the construction work. During the winter, he played hockey. At one stage in Winnipeg, he was a member of six teams.

"There were many days when I played hockey from ten o'clock in the morning until three o'clock the next morning," Red remembers. One winter he worked for Swift's Canadian Packers, and his primary job was to play for the company senior hockey team at a wage of $30 per week.

An economic depression gripped the country in 1922. By that time, Red was running a small construction company of his own. The contract was for moving dirt with a Fresno, on a railway right-of-way, south of Moose Jaw. A Fresno, named after the California town where it was invented, is shaped like a giant scoop-shovel about six feet wide and powered by a team of draught horses. A shortage of steel and depressed economic conditions brought railroad building to a halt, and Red Dutton's construction outfit along with it.

Reluctantly, Red sold the horses and paid his oats and hay bills. He still owed his day labourers $185, which would eventually have to be paid.

Back in Winnipeg, broke and unemployed, he lived with a sister, who fed him and advanced a dollar or two when she could afford it. He eagerly pitched in to help with household chores, in exchange for temporary room and board. It was a frustrating time – no money, no job prospects. But things can always get worse – and they did.

One day Red was removing the storm windows from the large old family home. He was high on a ladder, struggling with the lock on a stubborn window. The ladder began to move, and he knew he was in trouble.

"What am I going to do? Pitch the window and hang on to the frame, protect the window and jump?"

He decided to jump. He landed on the concrete sidewalk and broke both heels. That was in early April, and he was forced to spend three weeks in bed. Adding to his frustration was the nagging reality that he would miss the baseball season.

When the three weeks were up, he was up and moving on crutches. Red borrowed a few dollars from his sister to keep him in walk-around money. He spent the summer in Winnipeg, lamenting his bad luck.

Before the August shadows began to lengthen, his fortunes took a turn for the better. While Red was biding his time, working on the rehabilitation of his feet and ankles to get them into top skating condition, Pete Egan, a Portage La Prairie theatre manager, sought him out.

"'Where the hell have you been?' Pete asked me when he finally caught up to me. He had been authorized to offer me a contract to play professional hockey in Calgary. The offer included $500 right now, $500 more when I got to Calgary, $1,800 for the season and transportation both ways. I couldn't believe it," Red remembers. "I asked him to repeat the offer. 'Let's get that ticket right now,' I said. He gave me $500, and I was on my way to Calgary – no longer an amateur."

Red paid back his sister and some other small debts and landed in Calgary, where he had a highly successful season with the Calgary Canadians. The Canadians were in a four-team league with the Calgary Tigers, and two teams from Edmonton, the Dominions and the Eskimos.

The Canadians played their home games in the old Victoria Arena, on the site of Stampede Park. Lloyd Turner, the legendary hockey figure, managed the rink.

The following year, 1924, the Tigers and Canadians amalgamated and joined the Western Canada League, which included Edmonton, Regina, Saskatoon, Vancouver, Victoria, Seattle and Portland. The league was operated under the deft guidance of Frank and Lester Patrick, two of hockey's most prominent pioneers and promoters.

Lloyd Turner was the manager of the Calgary team, and Herb Gardiner paired with Dutton to form the most impenetrable defence in the league. It was an exhausting schedule, traveling long distances by train, sleeping in berths.

The Canadians went on to win the Stanley Cup after a bitterly fought final with Vancouver. The triumph established Dutton and Gardiner as two of hockey's most sought-after players. They carefully squirreled the press clippings which described, in the most florid terms, their heroics along the Calgary blue line. And they made a pact that henceforward, they were a packaged pair, and would not deal with hockey's flesh peddlers as individuals.

The National Hockey League, in Eastern Canada and the U.S., was expanding into the larger population centres, and many of the top Western Canada League players, with Dutton and Gardiner at the top of the list, were in demand.

"I told Herb one day that we're going to be sold – so let's make them pay for two of us; I won't sign, and you don't sign until we get the deal we want."

During that summer of 1925, Red, in partnership with his brother, Jack, was on a CPR branch line contract south of Moose Jaw. Herb Gardiner took a summer job on railroad construction east of Regina. Lester Patrick and Lloyd Turner were trying to get Dutton and Gardiner to sign with Cleveland.

Dutton played baseball almost every day, and made a lot of friends in the South Saskatchewan country. Among them was the railway station agent at Avonlea. One day, the station agent advised him by telephone, that two men – one tall with silver hair and the other quite stocky – were on the way to the camp on horseback.

"It was Patrick and Turner," Red recalls. "I didn't want to talk to them, so I grabbed a saddle pony and disappeared into the hills for two or three days." Red sat on a knoll about a mile away, and watched through high powered binoculars as Patrick and Turner talked to his brother Jack. He waited until they rode off.

Unable to nail Dutton to a commitment, the horsemen returned to Avonlea and went on east of Regina to talk with Gardiner. They duped Herb with the story that Dutton had signed. He came to terms readily, and became a member of the Cleveland Barons hockey team.

Merv "Red" Dutton · *Hockey Hall of Fame*

Meanwhile, Eddie Girard, Manager of the Montreal Maroons, contacted Dutton by telegram asking if he was available, and if so, could a meeting be arranged. Dutton then contacted his friend Gardiner, and learned of the subterfuge. He also learned that Cleveland was prepared to pay him the same salary as Gardiner — $3,500 for the season.

Red chose to delay a decision until his talks with Girard, who agreed to meet him in a Moose Jaw hotel room. Dutton drove to town in an ancient Ford truck and met Girard walking along the street.

"In the hotel, Eddie offered me $5,000 cash for signing, $5,000/year for three years, and an additional $1,000 if the Maroons made the playoffs, $1,000 if I'm selected to the all-star team and transportation for my wife and I both ways from Calgary."

Red had married a childhood sweetheart, the former Phyllis Wright of Russell, Manitoba. He was twenty-eight years old with two young sons and he wanted to establish a home.

"I liked the deal, but I decided to try him for $6,000 cash up front and $6,000 per year. He went for it without an argument, and I signed."

Dutton enjoyed the high wine of gladiatorial heroism during five seasons in Montreal. He was named an all-star NHL defenceman four times. His hell-for-leather skating style attracted people to rinks throughout the circuit.

Including bonuses, Red earned about $12,000 a season in Montreal. Most of the money was poured into Dutton Brothers Construction firm back in Calgary, which was under the direction of his younger brother, Jack. In 1933, the construction company, ravaged by the inactivity of the Depressions, went broke. Dutton persisted with hockey, which continued to pay off for him.

The stuttering New York Americans franchise needed a boost, and Eddie Girard was selected as the man to administer the therapy, Girard wanted Dutton as a cornerstone, and arranged a trade with New York for Lionel 'Big Train' Conacher. Red remembers New York as the zaniest period in this action-packed lifetime.

Shortly after his arrival in New York, the gravelly-voiced Girard succumbed to a lingering ailment which turned out to be throat cancer. The tragic departure of Girard created even more confusing times for the hapless Americans.

Part of the intrigue surrounding this anomalous franchise was the stigma surrounding its ownership. One of New York's most infamous racketeers, Bill O'Dwyer had somehow acquired the team and its assets without the league bothering to investigate his background. O'Dwyer's preoccupation centered around bootlegging, prohibition having created a highly buoyant market. His underworld activities also included horse racing and bookmaking.

He also had the reputation for being constantly short of money, at least as far as the hockey operations were concerned. The hockey team owed money for equipment, had difficulty in meeting player payrolls, and at the beginning of each season, hockey team management could barely scrape together the transportation money to assemble the players at training camp.

"Bullet" Joe Simpson succeeded Girard at the helm of the hockey team. After two tumultuous, riotous years, Joe passed it gladly to Dutton.

Dutton was unusual among hockey players. He continued to pursue construction projects in Western Canada, building for the future and saving his money. Construction was his security, hockey was his passion. And he skillfully used the publicity and the contacts gained throughout his hockey exploits to further his construction interests.

When Dutton became manager of the hockey team, he loaned O'Dwyer $20,000, secured by interests in race tracks in New York State and Florida.

The team played its home games in Madison Square Gardens, which owned the rival New York Rangers. Dutton used every promotional trick he knew to gain publicity and advantage over the Rangers, but it was too formidable a challenge even for him. For its final two years, the team moved to Brooklyn, as the Brooklyn Americans.

A combination of lawsuits and delinquent bills finally eliminated O'Dwyer from the picture, but the NHL Board of Governors felt the franchise was worth saving and took it over. Dutton was assigned to operate the team and was guaranteed the $20,000 owed him by O'Dwyer. Frank Calder, President of the NHL, advised Dutton that the governors had agreed to keep the Americans alive with Dutton at the helm.

"I said OK, as long as I can pay the bills and you get me the $20,000 from O'Dwyer."

NHL lawyers descended on O'Dwyer and foreclosed, which resulted in Dutton receiving a major interest in two race tracks.

"O'Dwyer begged me not to take his hockey team away from him," Dutton said.

Dutton vividly recalls the scene in O'Dwyer's secluded office, upstairs in a garage in downtown Manhattan. Art Chapman, the coach, accompanied Red as they approached it through an alley. They were on a mission to requisition money for team travel and operating expenses. The entrance was protected by two huge bodyguards.

"I'm the manager of the hockey team," I told one of the thugs on the door. "He allowed us into O'Dwyer's office, a huge room – the most memorable scene of my life. There was money everywhere in piles; tens, twenties, hundreds neatly stacked. O'Dwyer's rum runners were bringing in their money. In one corner there were three guys playing cards. O'Dwyer was sitting in the corner, exchanging money with three or four people lined up in front of his desk."

Dutton and Chapman joined the line, and in moments faced the team's owner with a detailed requisition for funds needed for skate laces, hockey sticks, meal money, hotel expenses, and return train fare to Chicago. O'Dwyer leafed out the specified amount in cash.

Dutton reflected on the moment. "While O'Dwyer was sitting there in the midst of all this money, all I could think of was my hockey players carrying NSF paycheques in their pockets and all the unpaid bills."

L–R: Merv Dutton
and Eddie Shore ·
Hockey Hall of Fame

"Don't take the hockey club away from me," was O'Dwyer's plea. "It's the only legitimate thing I ever had in my life."

With the backing of the league and Frank Calder, Dutton struggled with the American franchise until the end of 1941. Fighting in World War Two was at its most intense, and most of the top NHL players were in military uniform. Professional hockey's premier league was reduced to a gallant band of graying veterans, some eager teenagers and those who were medically unfit for military service.

An inability to find and recruit hockey players of NHL caliber, along with all its other woes, caused the final dissolution of the Americans at the end of the 1941 season.

The league governors, including Senator Donat Raymond of Montreal, Major Frederick McLaughlin of Chicago and James D. Norris, then of Detroit, promised Red that if he could build a rink in Brooklyn after the war, he would be granted an NHL franchise.

During his term as manager in New York, Red paid off about $200,000 in debts piled up by the profligate O'Dwyer. But the demands of wartime service on quality hockey players was the ultimate undoing of the Americans. Playing its last season as the Brooklyn Americans in 1941, Red bade a temporary farewell to hockey. It was agreed by the NHL governors that the team would fold, and that Dutton would be awarded a National Hockey League franchise, when normal hockey operations renewed after the war.

Red had returned to Calgary to pursue his interests in the construction industry, but the NHL governors called him in 1942.

League president Frank Calder had become ill, and with the support of the league governors, asked Dutton to fill in as President of the League on a temporary basis. Calder died a short time later.

Dutton was asked to take over the league presidency, but he was hesitant because of commitments to his construction partners back in Calgary.

By this time Dutton had teamed up with Reg Jennings, a "magnificent man" in Calgary, and they had formed Standard Gravel and Surfacing Ltd. Jennings could see the wisdom in Dutton taking on the NHL presidency, a position from which he would rub shoulders with prime ministers, cabinet ministers and the Canadian captains of finance and industry.

His credentials included membership in the Hockey Hall of Fame, of which he eventually became a board member.

Dutton held the NHL post until 1946, when he resigned in favour of Lt. Col. Clarence Campbell, M.B.E. The changing of the guard took place at the league's annual meeting in New York's Hotel Commodore. Among other items, Red reminded the governors of their promise of the franchise for Brooklyn.

The comment was greeted by a long silence.

Connie Smythe finally spoke, "There are complications Red. Madison Square Gardens wants two franchises."

"I've got people in Brooklyn ready to build – they're waiting for your approval," came Red's reply.

He then looked into each face, and each face was expressionless.

"I got the message," Red recalled. "Gentlemen," he said to the governors. "You can take your franchise and shove it."

He picked up his papers and stormed out of the room, and didn't attend another NHL hockey game until he dropped the first puck when the Calgary Flames came into the league in October 1980.

"DIRTY THIRTIES," for most Western Canadian pioneers, is a term recalling the oppressive miseries of drought, tough times, no work and no money.

There was the physical drought, a legacy of the endless periods of rainless, blistering summer, and the swirling dust storms which scattered the rich prairie top soil into grotesque roadside drifts. The drought drained the creative nutrients from the human spirit, and reduced proud, productive men to soul-destroying welfare.

And then there was the drought imposed by the tenets of Victorian Puritanism and fundamentalist bible interpretations which made it impossible for a man to find a drink of whiskey in a public place.

Whiskey drinkers were driven underground. A popular diversion for businessmen of the Depression was to establish a "snake room" in some obscure and private corner of his premises. It was a place where cronies, customers, suppliers and contacts of various kinds could get together for a few drinks from a "Syndicate" bottle of whiskey. During those austere times, three or four men would syndicate a dollar each on a bottle of "control board" whiskey, so called because it was marketed from an Alberta Liquor Control Board store.

A typical post-prohibition snake room was a major feature of Harry Oliver's machinery building at the corner of Eighth Avenue and Fourth Street South West in Calgary. It was located in the basement, out of sight of customers and the general public.

Reg Jennings and Harry Oliver were going over the possibilities for their newly-organized gravel crushing and surfacing business. It was late afternoon. The revitalizing warmth of the first swallow of "liquor board" rye was bringing new verve and enthusiasm to the tired muscles of a youthful Reg Jennings.

Suddenly and characteristically, a tall, sinewy redhead burst into the snake room, crowing about his good luck at the race track. It was Mervyn A. (Red) Dutton, and it was the first time Jennings ever laid eyes on him.

"I knew I was going to have some fun with Harry Oliver that day," Dutton remembered. Oliver owned a race horse that had been running for more than a year and had never won a race. "Somebody called me from Saskatoon," Red said, "and told me this nag, named Ya Fida, is long overdue and to get a bet down on him."

"I put $50 on the nose with the bookie, and Ya Fida wins going away as a ten to one shot. Anyway, I come in there telling Harry Oliver I made a score at the race track, but I don't tell him the name of the horse because I know he is the owner and probably didn't have a nickel on him," Red said.

"What was the horses's name?" asked Harry.

"Ya Fida," Dutton replied with an impish grin.

"Goddamn – I own that horse and I didn't have a nickel on him," Oliver said, pounding the table.

"I was laughing like hell when Harry said the least you could do is go and pick up a couple of crocks" Dutton recalled. "I put some money on the table and Harry asked Reg to slip over to the liquor store about a block away and pick up two bottles."

"That was the first day I ever met Reg Jennings, and while I didn't know it at the time, he was going to turn out to be the best guy I ever met in my life."

The following year Dutton Brothers had been awarded a contract to build the Calgary airport. Dutton Brothers broke the original ground at the site. Dutton's outfit was primarily a dirt-moving operation, and the gravel and surfacing portion of the contract had to be sublet. It turned out the first sub-contract went to Oliver Machinery, whose outfit was under the direction of Reg Jennings.

"We bid the job," Reg remembers, "and Dutton got the contract, based on his estimate plus our figures for the gravelling."

It was a transition time in the construction business. Horses were being phased out as a source of power and were being replaced by caterpillar tractors, elevating graders and large dirt moving machines known as Le Tourneaus. Until about 1936, there were still a few horse-drawn dump-wagons and the horse-powered slips and Fresnos used for moving dirt.

The Dutton crew began chewing at the Calgary airport in August 1937 and piled dirt until late November. A camp was set up near the gravel pit in the Nose Creek ravine.

"Dutton was away playing hockey, but we had a Christmas party in that workhouse right beside Nose Creek," Jennings said.

The Partners

The Jennings-Dutton working arrangement included all the appropriate ingredients for success. Jennings approached each project in a business-like fashion. He insisted on careful estimating, understanding specifications, efficiency in the employment of men and equipment. Most important, he was in constant search of new and more efficient ways of getting the work done.

Reg's five-foot seven-inch frame wasn't imposing on a construction crew, but he somehow gained the trust and affection of the men around him.

Dutton had contacts. Through his hockey career, he was well-known across Canada, and most doors were open to him. Ironically, he was not enthusiastic about contact work and preferred to be on the job site. As a construction supervisor, Dutton was impatient, hard-driving and did a lot of bellowing which, mercifully for the working crews, was largely muffled by the roar of the machines.

The first business arrangement of the partners was a highly successful one. The first phase of the airport job went smoothly and both organizations made money.

Dutton's crews moved the dirt and leveled the runways. Jennings followed up with the gravel, surfacing and finishing phase of the project. Reg first located a gravel pit in the Nose Creek Valley and crushed the gravel to a prescribed size. The gravel was delivered from the plant in trucks and spread on the runways.

"We mixed calcium chloride with the gravel and it became one of the first hard-surfaced runways in Western Canada," Jennings said.

The contract began in 1937, and in 1938 it was expanded to include an extension and a tarmac in front of the original terminal building.

A year later Harry Oliver was dead, but Jennings continued as general manager of the gravel and surfacing business until well into 1940 when he made arrangements to buy the business from the estate.

Jennings' original mentor in Great Falls, Jay McLaughlin, was in high gear with his own construction operations, and offered to finance Reg in the purchase of the Oliver equipment from the trust company representing the estate.

Reg was keen to consummate a deal. He had operated the equipment for a little more than two years and had cleared $215,000 on behalf of the Oliver estate.

"I wanted it to be a Canadian operation, and I wanted Dutton for a partner rather than bringing in the Americans," Jennings said.

"I wrote Dutton in New York, but he was so damn busy trying to keep his hockey team afloat he didn't answer me," Reg said.

H. A. Howard wanted to get the deal cleaned up and get the trust company out of the construction business. "I came very close to following up with Jay McLaughlin when I didn't hear from Dutton. I was under pressure to make a move. On February 13, 1941, Jennings fired the following letter to New York, from his home on Westmount Road in Calgary.

"Dear Red,

A few lines to let you know we are starting to get itchie feet and thinking about spring work.

The past two weeks have been just like spring, in fact close to summer weather, with the mercury up around 60 degree mark, so you can see we have every reason to be getting restless. However it is turning colder tonight, and would not be surprised if we get a spell of winter.

I am enclosing cost statements I made up in connection with the Airdrie work, which I thought might be of interest to you. By adding the net profit of the three statements together, you get the total profit made on the blacktop, consolidated gravel base and crushing of the rock for the ditches, which aggregate close to $31,000 as you see, so all in all turned out to be a fairly profitable job. From a competitive stand point, I do not believe it advisable to use these figures as actual costs, as a good number of the items can be cut a considerable figure and still show a substantial profit. However, this is something I will discuss with you on our next meeting, as it would not be practical to try and outline them in a letter.

Have you heard anymore on the Shepard job? Last night's (Calgary) Herald announced the location of the relief fields for Penhold and Claresholm, Penhold having one at Innisfail and the other at Bowden, Claresholm having one at Woodhouse the first siding south and the other near Pultney the first siding north. On the Shepard job, which in my mind is the best looking job, I have been wondering how this man Doncaster stands. While he still has some work to finish on the Lethbridge field, from what I can find out he would still finish his gravelling and blacktop in time to step into the Shepard job, as his grading work at Lethbridge does not amount to an awful lot, so that by the time he finished grading at Shepard (providing he got the job) his gravelling and blacktop outfit, (which incidentally happens to be Jenkins outfit) would hit there at about the right time, according to my calculations. Possibly you have these details, but in case you have not, I thought it worthwhile to bring it to your attention as this Shepard job looks like a nice proposition to me.

Possibly Fred has told you that it is the intention of Mrs. Oliver and Howard to dispose of the Oliver equipment this spring. Before making any other moves, I have been wondering if you would be interested in the proposition. Fred mentioned it to me a short time ago, but has not mentioned it since. He left for the Coast yesterday morning, and as Howard has informed me he would like to get cleaned up around the 15th of March, I thought I would write you about the deal. While I have been offered several propositions lately in connection with taking the business over, I felt, that in view of our past satisfactory dealings, I would ask you if you were interested. There will be considerable work in and around the city (Calgary) this year, and in view of the fact that hard surfaced roads are just in their infancy in this country, the business I believe has a good future. Confidentially during the 17 months ending December 31st, while I was running the show for the estate, we cleared $53,000 plus $18,000 worth of equipment purchased, this of course being the operating profits before making any deduction for depreciation or income taxes, but taking care of all operating costs, overhead, etc., this just gives you a rough picture of the possibilities of the business. While it might be said that a lot of our work last year was not competitive work, I can assure you that some of the prices we received were lower than on a competitive basis, however our good friend Jenkins probably got the benefit of some of the differences, however that is outside the point. If you are at all interested Red, I would appreciate hearing from you at an early date, in order that I may guide myself accordingly.

> With kind regards,
> Sincerely yours,
>
> Reg"

Don McPhail on Pay Scraper; joined Standard in 1947

"I received no reply, so in about March 1941, I formed Standard Gravel and Surfacing company, taking in Fred Owens, one of Dutton's partners, because I couldn't handle it alone."

Ross Henderson, a chartered accountant, was an officer in the original company, but he hadn't any money invested.

Dutton returned from the hockey wars later in the spring, claiming no knowledge of the letter, but enthusiastic that Dutton Brothers should have a piece of the action in Standard Gravel and Surfacing.

War contracts were starting to materialize all over the country. Dutton Brothers were involved in a joint venture in Winnipeg with Bob Paget of Assiniboia Engineering Company.

"When we got into the negotiations, it turned out that a full partnership was too much for Dutton Brothers," Reg said. "We reorganized the company, Dutton Brothers took a third, Paget took a third, and I took a third," Reg said. "From there on we just started to roll and grow."

Paget was an ex-CPR engineer who had worked with Dutton's father on railroad construction in Manitoba. Red had worked under him as a boy.

Although business was good, the partners of the new company were far apart in their fundamental beliefs about business.

"They were at loggerheads from the day we formed the bloody company," Jennings said. "Paget wanted to go out and buy a piece of equipment, and Dutton's brother Jack, who was very conservative, would object because he didn't believe in going into debt.

"Well hell, we were moving so fast, we had to expand the equipment, we couldn't stop. I had the support of Paget and the support of Merv, but the other partners in Dutton Brothers were constantly holding back.

"Jack and Fred Owens were both fine fellows but very, very conservative. They had never run anything very large and they couldn't understand this rapid expansion. They just wanted to remain on a nice even keel, maybe making forty or fifty thousand bucks a year – well, you can't go very far in the construction business making forty or fifty thousand bucks a year – you just stay in one little puddle.

"Paget was different, he was always prepared to say, 'O.K. friends, let's go out and buy a new crushing plant.' He even frightened me sometimes, because I wanted to be damn sure we were in good shape with our bank credits."

Dutton came storming in one day and said: "I'm going to get Jack and Fred Owens out of this thing." It wasn't long after that a deal was made to buy up the shares owned by Jack Dutton and Owens. Dutton then wanted to buy up Paget's shares.

Reg remembers the tension. "Dutton wouldn't talk to Paget – they were at loggerheads then and weren't speaking to each other."

The company was structured with Jennings as the managing director and Dutton as President. "We made him President so we could use his name when we went to Ottawa looking for work. I actually ran the whole damn affair, and nobody bothered me too much outside the fact we needed to borrow money for expansion. I would have to go to all of those guys to get the financial guarantees signed for the bank," Reg said. "Dutton didn't have the heart to force anybody out, he always wanted me to do the dirty work."

The company became more stable financially, which eventually allowed Dutton and Jennings to borrow sufficient money to buy up the Paget share. It was at this time that Dutton Brothers passed out of existence and Merv and Reg became equal partners in Standard Gravel and Surfacing.

Dutton & Jennings:
the Standard Saga
❋

During the 1930s, the name "Red" Dutton was spoken in the same reverent tones among sports enthusiasts as would be used in later years when speaking of Mario Lemieux or Wayne Gretzky.

The name "Red" Dutton was a door-opener. Although Dutton periodically ran into important government dignitaries during his hockey playing days, it wasn't until well past retirement that he developed the contacts and made life-long friendships in Ottawa.

The first foray into the unknown mysteries of the nation's capital was very early in World War II. It was early summer and Dutton had returned from his duties as manager of the New York Americans.

Reg and Merv had learned of the establishment of the Commonwealth Air Training Plan, which was being organized to train fighter and bomber crews for all of the allied nations. It would mean dozens of airports to be built all across Western Canada. "We'd better get in on this," Merv told Reg one day as they talked strategy in Standard's tiny head office.

The original business office was in the Lancaster Building on Eighth Avenue and Second Street South West in downtown Calgary. There were two small rooms. One was a working area, with storage space for stationary and a secretary-bookkeeper's desk; the other contained back-to-back offices – one for Jennings, one for Dutton. Even to the end, and the ultimate sale of their holdings, Dutton and Jennings had back-to-back desks in their Chinook Centre office in South Calgary.

"How are you going to get us in on these airports?" asked Reg.

"I don't know, but I'll figure something out," replied Dutton.

Dutton devised a strategy which called for taking along a respected Liberal with him to Ottawa. He believed that identifying with a recognizable party stalwart might provide an advantage in the quest for construction contracts.

He chose Harold Millican, a Calgary lawyer, who handled Standard's legal affairs and who had recently been defeated as a Liberal candidate in Calgary. Millican was also a lifelong crony of the construction company's principal shareholders.

"I think only four people voted for him," Dutton said. "Himself, his wife, me and somebody else."

Harold suffered defeat gracefully, as well as the incessant ribbing from Dutton and Jennings, and agreed to accompany Dutton to Ottawa.

Millican's only solid contact was Ford Pratt, a senior civil servant and father of Bill Pratt, who was later to become an important figure in the development of Standard and who eventually became general manager of the Calgary Exhibition and Stampede.

Receptionist Julie Crow, 1974

"We wandered around Ottawa, from one office to another, trying to find the right place to start asking the questions," Dutton said.

Neither he, nor Jennings, nor Millican for that matter, had any experience in negotiating government contracts. Up until that time, the only contact they had made with government had been with the engineer on the Calgary airport.

Eventually, after two days of wandering blindly, Millican caught up with his contact. Ford Pratt was Executive Assistant to the Minister in charge of Indian Affairs, and received the two Westerners warmly. After a brief discussion with Pratt, the two Westerners were advised to make an appointment with Herb Edgett, the federal purchasing agent.

"How do I do that?" Dutton asked.

"Just go to his office, knock on the door and say you would like to speak with Mr. Edgett," was Pratt's advice. "Talk to him, that's the only way to do it – go in there and tell him what you can do."

Fascinated by the challenge of learning to deal with the mysterious world of politicians and the public service, Dutton rose early the following morning, determined to find his way through the bureaucracy, and ultimately to the source of government construction contracts.

"I got myself all spit and polished and found my way to the purchasing agent's office," Dutton said.

"Do you have an appointment?" asked an efficient and unsmiling receptionist.

"No," he said, "but I came down from Calgary and would like to see Mr. Edgett."

Fortunately Edgett recognized the name. He had apparently remembered Dutton in connection with the original Calgary airport contract.

Dutton explained that he had learned of the program to develop the airports which would form the backbone of the Commonwealth Air Training Plan. He suggested that Standard Gravel and Surfacing was ready, willing and able, with men and equipment to handle any work on the project which might come available.

Edgett explained that the initial emphasis was to be in the East, and that very little thought had been given to the West, although as the plan developed there were several airports scheduled to be built in the West.

"Will it come under your department?" Dutton asked.

"It will come under the engineering department," he replied.

Almost as an afterthought he asked Dutton if he knew C.D. Howe.

"No, I don't know him," Dutton replied, "but I certainly know who he is, and he was a friend of my father's."

Edgett then advised him to contact Bill Bennett, the Deputy Minister in Mr. Howe's Department of Munitions and Supply.

"Tell Bennett who you are, explain that you are interested in the airport contracts and explain your capabilities in manpower and equipment," Edgett suggested. "And if you don't get anywhere over there, come back."

Dutton was feeling better about his first business trip to Ottawa as a construction man. He was impressed with the open reception in Edgett's office, and the helpful way in which the purchasing agent dealt with him.

"He asked me back. That was a good sign – that was what I wanted – he asked me back."

He contacted Bennett by telephone, introduced himself and explained his mission. In those days he always referred to himself as "Red" Dutton, never as Merv, as he did in later years.

"Oh yeah, not 'Red' Dutton the hockey player?" Bennett asked.

"The same," Red replied.

"Well, come on over, let's talk," he said.

Dutton thought he detected a note of interest in hockey in Bennett's voice. Then he thought it might be good strategy to exclude Millican from the initial visit.

"I better just do this alone," he told Harold. "I'm in now – I've got the foot in the door and I don't want anybody to say something that will upset anything."

"Harold was a good lawyer, but he didn't know much about hockey, and he sure as hell didn't know much about construction. I'm dubious about lawyers, sometimes they can really get their foot in their mouths," Dutton said.

He left Harold in the room at the Chateau Laurier and made his way to Bennett's office on Parliament Hill. Again, he was welcomed warmly. It turned out there wasn't much hockey discussed at all, and Dutton explained in careful detail about the organization he and Reg Jennings had built up. He was particularly emphatic about their interest in getting involved in some of the construction connected with the air training plan.

Part way through the conversation, the door opened, and in walked the man who would be credited by history as one of the principal architects of Canada's modern industrial structure, Clarence Decatur Howe.

Bennett waited until Howe was settled in the inner office, and then followed. In a moment, Dutton was beckoned to the minister's office.

After as brief introduction, Howe asked: "Are you the son of W.A. Dutton?"

"Yes," answered Red.

"I knew your father very well. I built all the elevators at Fort William, and your father was building railroads in that district at the time."

It was an awkward time for Dutton. No man could intimidate him in a hockey rink, and no construction job was too large to handle. But making polite social talk in front of a national political figure was not Dutton's strong suit.

He decided to come right to the point. "Mr. Howe," he said. "I'm a western contractor, and our firm – Standard Gravel and Surfacing – would like to get some of the work in Western Canada when the Commonwealth Air Training Plan contracts come up."

Howe's reply was equally terse.

"We'll put you on the list, and when the work comes out there, you will be contacted," Howe said.

"Thank you very much," Red replied, as he began backing toward the door.

In the outer office, Dutton thanked Bennett profusely for arranging the meeting. Before he got away, he learned that his hunch was right about Bennett's interest in hockey. He remained for more than an hour exchanging hockey stories with the deputy minister. It turned out that Bennett was an uncompromising fanatic on the subject of hockey, and that he was a close crony of King Clancy.

Dutton then returned to Edgett's office, in the belief that courtesy demanded he report on his good fortune to meet Mr. Howe and to develop an easy rapport with Bennett.

L–R: Fred Schutz, Audrey Smith (Secretary) and Reg Jennings

Dutton returned to the Chateau in a buoyant mood. In his conversations, he learned that Mr. Howe's department had a lot to do with whose names appeared on the contractor's list. It was Edgett who was in charge of maintaining the list.

He suggested to Millican that they stick around Ottawa for another day or two, and invite Edgett to lunch so he could get to know him even better.

Edgett agreed to come to lunch the following day, and joined Red and Harold in the dining room of the Chateau Laurier. It was an easy, leisurely time with Millican contributing the pleasant conversational dimension of a man rooted and reared in the traditions of Western Canadian life.

"Are you fellows committed for the afternoon?" Edgett asked, as the lunch hour stretched on toward one thirty.

"Nothing at all on for this afternoon," Dutton said. "We're catching the train at eight o'clock."

"I think it would be worthwhile for you to meet one of our senior engineers in the engineering department," Edgett said.

They returned to Edgett's office, just off Wellington Street, where they were introduced to a man whose first name was Ted. It was to be an object lesson in East-West relations in Canada, and a symbolic moment that irritated Dutton for the rest of his life.

"This guy was an EASTERNER, and as far as he was concerned, Westerners couldn't do anything at all," Red said.

"We'll be starting up in the West very soon," the man said, referring to the start-up of the Commonwealth Air Training Plan. "But we'll be sending Eastern contractors out there because you people don't have the equipment."

That did it. The engineer had discovered the quickest way to ignite Dutton's short fuse. It was a moment when Dutton called upon all the patience and diplomacy buried deep within his crusty exterior.

"That's not so – that's just not so," said Dutton in a restrained roar. "We have all the equipment. We have as much equipment as those people down east, and what we haven't got to get the job done, we can get in a helluva hurry."

"We're in a position to build those airports. And what's more, if you're going to ship those Eastern contractors out west when there's plenty of work in the East for them, then I think you're doubling up on yourself," Dutton added.

"It was quickly very obvious," Dutton said, "he took a dire dislike to me, and I took an equally dire dislike to him."

After the meeting, and after Millican had exercised his soothing influence on the raging redhead, Dutton decided it would be prudent to stay over and discuss the East-West conflict with Bill Bennett.

A phone call to Bennett's office about four o'clock that afternoon, with the suggestion they contact King Clancy and arrange dinner the following evening, was received with an enthusiastic response.

"That fellow Bennett would talk hockey any time he got the chance," Dutton said. "I couldn't find Clancy anywhere," Dutton remembers, "but Bennett and I had dinner together anyway, and had a good time telling hockey stories."

Fred Chatelain joined Standard in 1947

Dutton also managed to describe his concern about the policy of shipping Eastern contractors to perform jobs in the West.

"Don't worry about it – I can promise you that you don't need to worry about it – when the work comes up you will be considered," Bennett reassured Dutton.

Dutton and Millican caught the west-bound train the following night. Dutton was considerably wiser and exceedingly pleased that he had established contact with Edgett, Bennett, and most important of all, C.D. Howe.

Both Jennings and Dutton would become more closely attached to these three men as the years rolled by.

The initial contact was to be the beginning of one of the most dramatic Horatio Alger stories of Canadian business – certainly Western Canadian business.

It wasn't long after the first Ottawa trip that Dutton and Jennings were awarded one contract, then another, and ultimately the almost impossible challenge of the Woodcock job in the wilds of British Columbia.

There were to be many trips to Ottawa, and each time Dutton or Jennings, and often both, would touch base with their important contacts — all of whom were to become close personal friends.

Along with the airports came large-scale contracts for construction of hangars. Dutton and Jennings were equipped for this eventuality with the establishment of Burns and Dutton Construction.

The first hangar that came up was approximately $6 million, and the bidding had been against Poole, Miller Construction and several others.

Jennings carefully supervised the estimating and prepared a bid on the job. Dutton's part was to be in Ottawa on the closing date, where he could hand deliver the bid, the deposit cheque and the necessary bonds. The bids would be opened about 10:00 a.m. and by noon the successful bidder would be announced.

"We weren't told what the other bids contained — only whether we were successful or not," Dutton said. "I wanted that hangar real bad," Dutton said, "because our building company had grown to the point where it was capable of taking on large jobs."

At noon on the prescribed day, Dutton received a call from a contact in the purchasing agent's office informing him that his company had been successful on the contract.

"That was terrific — a $6 million contract — that would really put Burns and Dutton in business. After I got the news, I went for lunch and had a few drinks to celebrate the good fortune. In the meantime, I phoned Reg to tell him the good news."

The period of elation was to be short-lived.

At four o'clock Dutton received a phone call from the purchasing agent's office advising him to get over there to protect the bid because someone had come in with an alternate.

"What do you mean putting in an alternative, the bids are closed," Dutton argued.

The voice on the telephone advised Dutton that an alternative bid had arrived, cutting the price of the hangar by more than one million dollars.

"I was sick," Dutton said. "And then I got mad."

He headed directly for C.D. Howe's office, where he was intercepted by Bill Bennett.

"I've got to see Mr. Howe," Dutton demanded.

"What's this all about?" Bennett asked.

Dutton then explained his concern about the alternate bid, and suggested that in fairness he should be allowed to discuss it with the Minister and tender a revised bid.

It was common knowledge that Howe studied all the bids on major jobs under his department's jurisdiction and that it was his signature that ultimately awarded the contract.

It was almost five o'clock before Dutton was allowed into the meticulously organized office of the minister. Even after the cooling-off session with Bennett, he was in a highly-agitated state.

"What can I do for you?" asked Mr. Howe.

Again Dutton explained his concern over the alternate bid.

"We spent a lot of money on that bid, and I feel if you are going to accept an alternate bid from another contractor, you should accept an alternate bid from us," Dutton said. "I don't think that's asking too much."

"Was that the Edmonton hangar job?" the minister asked quietly.

Dutton nodded his head.

"It's too late, Red."

"What do you mean, it's too late," came the reply. "There was nothing in the specifications that called for an alternative bid."

"Oh well, don't worry about that," Mr. Howe said. "Something else will come up, and we'll make up for it. There will be lots more work, and we'll see to it that you get plenty of work to keep your outfits busy."

"That's not the point – this is very unfair," Dutton argued.

It was becoming obvious that his persistence in this office was getting under the minister's skin.

"Dutton," he roared, "you're walking around here like a chicken with its head cut off – and if you don't get out of this office right now, I'm going to throw you out."

Runway paving, Calgary Airport

"You can throw me out," replied Dutton. "But if you do, I'll be back tomorrow."

"Don't you dare come back here tomorrow," roared the Minister. "And don't you dare challenge my right to save the government of Canada one million dollars."

Dutton knew he was defeated, and he turned on his heel and retreated. It was one of many incidents in Howe's office over the years. Years later, both men mellowed slightly, and were able to laugh about their earlier altercations.

New 295 Pay Scraper, 1965

Jennings and Dutton received some satisfaction from that particular hangar job sooner than they expected. They learned through a contact in Edgett's office that the job cost the government more than $7.5 million before they were finished. A Belgian architect had apparently designed a new type of spanning arch and it failed, and most of the structure had to be rebuilt.

Howe's word was good, and soon he called and assigned the Woodcock airport with no strings attached.

In a later incident, the airport at Regina came up for bid. Dutton was in Winnipeg and the call came to Reg, who was in his Calgary office. Reg relayed the message to Winnipeg that Mr. Howe wanted someone in Ottawa to discuss the Regina job.

It was unusual for the Minister to discuss bids; he either approved or rejected them.

Several weeks prior to the phone call, the Regina airport came up for bid about the same time as a big extension was called for the Calgary airport. Dutton and Jennings worked out a game plan they thought might confuse the opposition.

They arrived in Regina with a large entourage of engineers and other experts, making it as obvious as possible they were keen to get the Regina contract. Their real interest was the Calgary airport, where they knew every inch of ground, and the men and equipment were all in place. It was a well-played charade, with the Standard Gravel contingent marching about the prairie that was to become the Regina airport while the Mannix, Poole and Wells people watched with bemused interest.

The Jennings-Dutton strategy was to not bid on Regina, and hope the competition would get so involved in Regina they would forget about the Calgary airport.

It turned out that only two contractors bid on the Regina job, and C.D. Howe was suspicious. The bids also appeared to the Minister to be inordinately high.

Again Dutton was greeted by his friend Bennett, and again, after a short time, he was ushered into Mr. Howe's office. He shook hands with the Minister.

"Hello Red, how are you?"

"Fine, thank you sir, and you?"

"Now," he said, without further hesitation, "why didn't you bid that Regina airport?"

"Well Mr. Howe, it was our information that a big extension to the Calgary airport was coming up. Reg and I went to Regina with a crew of men and began estimating it, we concluded we were better off in Calgary where we could concentrate our men and equipment."

"Are you sure there was no collusion?" asked Mr. Howe.

Dutton was taken off balance with the suggestion of collusion. He was determined to convince the Minister there had been no conversation at any time with any of the other contractors concerning collusion.

Apparently the minister was convinced after the discussion that Dutton and Jennings had not discussed strategy with other contractors.

Before Dutton left the office, Howe issued a stern warning.

"Red, if I ever catch you in collusion with any of these contractors, I'll break you and that outfit of yours so you'll never earn another dollar as long as you live."

Dutton said no more, but he knew that relations with the Minister's office were not in jeopardy because the Jennings-Dutton creed demanded they avoid collusion in the contracting business.

"Hockey was good to Dutton," said Reg, "and in a sense hockey was good to me, because of my acquaintance with him. His hockey gave him a great entrée to a lot of doors that we wanted to knock on. C.D. Howe was just tickled to death – if he was in a good humor – when Dutton would come in and sit down and discuss hockey. But Dutton was very impatient. I used to go to C.D. Howe's office with him, and I got to know him well enough that if you went into his office and he looked up saw you coming in and spoke to you in a pretty civil tone, it was a time to sit there and talk to him.

"If he'd put his feet upon the desk and get a cigarette out, then you should stay and talk hockey. But Jesus, Dutton would get impatient you see – he just wanted to get in and get out. He actually never liked doing that type of work, you see, he didn't like making the contact work at all. In fact, in later years, I did an awful lot of it myself. He just didn't like it."

THE HEART OF THE GREAT DEPRESSION during the dirty thirties was a difficult period for construction firms in Canada. Large scale construction projects were a rarity — particularly in the West.

A scattered few diesel-powered graders and tractors were employed by the well-established contractors, but the large, handsome, heavy-duty Clydesdales and Percherons had not yet been rendered obsolete by automotive power.

As the Dutton-Jennings era of construction began to evolve during the early months of World War II, so did the style and *modus operandi* of the two partners. Dutton was keen for the company to grow and flourish, and his big barrel-chested ego demanded big, monumental contracts. Jennings was constantly amused. Through more than forty years of close association with Dutton's ebullience, Reg, whose vision extended far beyond the horizon on the technical-managerial side of the construction game, was fully appreciative of Dutton's unquenchable desire to take on big projects.

Dutton's responsibility was to keep up his government contacts, bring in the big jobs. It was Jennings' responsibility to figure out how to get them done – on time – efficiently – and with a profit.

During the period 1942 through 1946, Dutton was largely engrossed in his responsibilities as President of the National Hockey League. His major contribution during this period was to establish contacts for the company.

Meanwhile, Reg was obsessed with finding better ways to get things done. He looked for more efficiency, more speed, and above all, he believed that the available equipment during the period was cumbersome, slow and difficult to operate.

Reg possessed zero tolerance for inefficiency. A basic tranquil temperament shrouded his frustrations with a permanent smile, and the mischievous dancing eyes. Time lost moving a camp, a crushing plant and an asphalt plant from one location to another was more than his saintly temperament could bear.

In the construction business, the summer months, and clear, sunny days were a major ally. Every warm dry day was money in the bank if the equipment was working. When a project was completed, it was accepted practice to dissemble the crushing plant and the asphalt plant into their countless complex parts. Like giant erector sets, the parts were numbered and stacked on a low flatbed according to a system unfathomable to the layman's eye. The tear-down process normally took about a week. The parts were moved to the next location, unloaded and put back together again. The reconstruction occupied another week of valuable production time.

Reg, seething on the sidelines, watched these tear-down and build-up sessions in an ever accelerating state of irritation.

"Why not just put wheels under the goddamn plant, and pull it to the next location with a 'cat'?" The thought became an obsession with Reg. The mechanics of the idea began to take shape as he discussed it with Frank Logelin and others on the crew.

Horse-drawn Fresno, 1920s

Within days of that meeting, Reg ordered a change in procedure. He supervised the crew while they placed industrial grade jacks under the asphalt plant and elevated it high enough for a long flatbed riding on eight huge rubber-tired wheels to slide under it. The plant, now on wheels, was hooked to a big truck and moved up the road twenty miles to the next location. Reg smiled as he recalled the joy of gaining two weeks of production time.

"We used to move that plant during the night, and be working on another airport the following day," Dutton said.

Arnold Berg, a young employee with a baby face and honey-blond hair, remembers Reg's determination to increase productivity and efficiency.

"Reg could tell whether the gravel crusher was running at 250 or 300 revolutions per minute from 100 yards away just by listening to it," Berg said.

Berg joined Reg as a travel truck dump man and time keeper in 1938, when Jennings was still operating Harry Oliver's gravel equipment.

"I heard there might be a chance to get on with Reg at the Calgary airport, after I was laid off from a government job," Berg said. "I jumped on the street car downtown and rode out to the Tuxedo loop at thirty-second avenue north west. From there, I walked to the original gravel pit and camp, located by the railway tracks in Nose Creek Valley, about 48th Avenue. It was a five-mile walk, but it turned out to be the most profitable trip I ever made in my life. It was there in that dusty, primitive, old construction camp that I first met Reg Jennings."

Probably the most significant technological breakthrough credited to Reg was the invention of the continuous mix process for asphalt. Berg explained that the traditional method of mixing asphalt involved weighing each of the ingredients — sand, fine rock and coarse rock, and moving it in individual lots to the batch plant where the oil was added.

The weighing process required hoppers and vertical bins arranged in a row high enough for a truck to drive under. Each hopper had a trip lever which required a man to operate. The process didn't seem right to Reg. It was slow, awkward and the men on the levers spent more than half their time idle.

Slowly and inevitably, he developed a new idea. Why weigh the ingredients each time? Why not establish how much volume a ton of sand occupies, and feed the batcher on a volume basis? Then his fertile mind conceived a new arrangement. Bins could be lined up side by side along a conveyor belt. The gates on the bins could be timed to open automatically at regular intervals and drop precisely the same amount of sand, fine rock and coarse rock on the belt at the same time. The belt carried the materials to the mixer on a continuous cycle and the hot asphalt would pour out in a consistent texture ready for the surfacing machines.

Reg experimented until he got everything performing the way he wanted it, with the three gates pouring precise amounts of material on the belt. His innovative nature and persistence produced the first continuous mix plant in Canada.

The Pioneer Manufacturing Company in Minneapolis assigned a young engineer named Don to work with Reg on refinement of his idea. Pioneer paid Standard Gravel a development fee in exchange for the right to patent the idea. Reg's invention was the prototype for hundreds of similar machines that would be built by Pioneer.

"I'll never forget the way we worked on that first continuous mix plant," Reg said. "My God, it was day and night – dust and dirt, and I don't know how the hell we lived through all that goddamn dust and dirt. We ate it for days on end. We would run through dry material, and the dust was something terrible. We improvised bins – we improved conveyor belts – we improvised drawing plants – all kinds of damn stuff. But you couldn't buy it, because it wasn't on the market."

It was a benchmark, technological breakthrough for the surfacing industry, but there remained one major hurdle which involved acceptance by the government. The quality of the asphalt and the method by which it was made was under constant supervision by government engineers. Reg instructed Dutton to deal with the government people and get approval for the portable, continuous mix asphalt plant.

The supervising engineer was a former oil company engineer who had worked most of his life in eastern refineries on asphalt projects before his career move to government. He was the same man Dutton had crossed swords with earlier on the contentious issue of sending Eastern contractors west to build the airports. Dutton described him as an overweight, slovenly creature. The engineer had an insatiable appetite for expensive food and an uncontrollable thirst for somebody else's booze.

L–R: Elmer "Lefty" Myrose, Metro Boyhachuck, Erhard Nickle,
in the coffee room, 1968

Dutton arranged for a suite in Calgary's York Hotel, and invited the man for dinner and drinks.

"I hated to sit down at the table with him," Dutton said. "He had the table manners of a pig. We had to get along with him — there was no other way — he could shut us down."

The engineer devoured mountainous portions of prime rib of beef and inhaled large volumes of booze financed by the construction company. Dutton coddled the government man's ego and used his persuasive skills to convince the man of the virtues of Reg's magnificent new development. Still the man ate and drank and frowned.

Dutton, nobly hiding his contempt, was determined to gain the man's confidence.

Finally, between mouthfuls, the government engineer said, "It will never work, and I won't approve it. You can't maintain consistent specifications with an arrangement like that."

Dutton was enraged, but he maintained a grip on himself.

"I goddamn near picked him up and threw him out the window," Dutton said. "But I knew it was time to go over his head, and make a trip to Ottawa," he recalled.

He contacted Bill Bennett, who arranged a meeting in Ottawa with C.D. Howe, and the question of approval was easily resolved.

Reg is credited with being the first Canadian to haul the heavy oil for asphalt in a tank trunk. It had traditionally been hauled by railway tank cars equipped with tank heaters capable of keeping the molasses-like substances in a liquid state.

Sam Cavanagh, the nephew of a friend of Reg, had mustered out of the air force and was looking for ways to get established in the trucking business. Reg experimented with tanker trucks and tank heaters until he had a workable model ready for the road. Then he backed young Cavanagh, who began hauling the heavy oil from the Gulf and Imperial refineries in Calgary, Wainwright and Lloydminster.

Reg could see that road and highway paving was going to be big business in Western Canada when the war was over. "We looked into highway paving and road grading, and before we were through we paved every mile of the TransCanada Highway from Medicine Hat, through Banff to the British Colombia border," Reg said. "Then we laid the first pavement from Banff to Jasper and the first pavement from Banff to Radium."

Dutton and Jennings produced the first light-weight aggregate in Canada. Making aggregate involves exposing shale to intense heat until it explodes. The exploding gives the effect of puffing it up like popcorn, making it much less dense and much lighter. The operation used shale from DeWinton.

Chick Thorssen and Bev Monkman built the business for Dutton and Jennings and helped develop the markets. Frank Logelin ran the operations and Jim McKendry worked alongside on the technical end.

Bob Hardy, a young engineer on the Standard staff, mentioned the idea of light-weight aggregate to Reg one day on one of the jobs. Hardy's interest was in road construction, but he had read somewhere about light-weight aggregate and believed it to be the coming thing.

"I didn't know what the hell light-weight aggregate was," Reg said.

Hardy explained that its main use was in concrete building blocks. He predicted there would come a day when brick layers would no longer work with the old, dense sand and gravel blocks, because they were too heavy.

Reg took a trip to Ventura, California to visit a light-weight plant, and another to Napa Valley, California, where a man named "Swede" Johnson was making the aggregate from pumice.

Johnson worked with Reg in helping him to understand the principles involved and provided him with all the information he needed to get into the light-weight aggregate business.

"The only thing that remained to be done when I got home," Reg said, "was to raise $600,000 to build a plant."

Which he did in the spring of 1950. The new company was called Peerless Rock Products.

Reg made a deal with Ed Jefferies, a competitor in the concrete business, to purchase the light-weight aggregate as the feed stock for his concrete block plant. Jefferies turned down Reg's offer of a partnership opportunity in the aggregate plant, but agreed to buy the product. Light-weight concrete blocks found a highly receptive market in the early fifties.

"It looked so good, we finally ended up buying Jefferies block plant," Reg said with a grin.

One of Reg's earliest inventions was the automatic gravel dryer. It was accepted practice that gravel had to be perfectly dry in the asphalt mixing process. In the pioneer days, drying gravel was a primitive, back-breaking process. Legions of workmen, with large shovels, attacked a rained-soaked mountain of gravel. They would turn it over and over by the shovel full in the hot sun until it was dry.

It was more than Reg could bear to watch able men being paid good money to perform such an unproductive task as drying gravel.

"There was no such thing as a gravel dryer on the market, so we had to build one," Reg said. He recalled from his days in the Turner Valley oilfield, the huge storage drums, about twelve feet in diameter, and about thirty feet high.

Reg conceived the idea of laying the drum on its side, and hooking it up to power so it would rotate. Inside, he welded a series of flat-iron baffles that would stir the gravel constantly as the drum rotated. In one end, he affixed a large fan and rigged up a burner in front of the fan which would produce a steady flow of heat.

At the other end, he hooked up a large suction device which would draw the heat through the rotating gravel, and at the same time, draw off the dust. The dust in those days, before environmental controls, was blown off into the prairie atmosphere.

It was bound to save time, money and energy, but Reg was stumped for weeks searching for a workable mechanism to rotate the fan. He eventually conceived the idea of welding a twelve-foot diameter cog wheel, which he found in a scrap heap, to the outside of the drum. From there, he meshed it with a gear on a long drive-shaft. It was all put-together in Standard's shop, and moved out to the De Winton airport job for a maiden run.

"Dutton started the damn thing up, and there was so much soot and dust, we jammed the fan solid," Reg said. "We got so much soot from the flame, which had not yet been adjusted properly, it packed solidly into the fan.

"Well, poor old Dutton, he threw his hat on the ground and stamped on it, and said 'to hell with this'. He took off to Banff for a couple of days to cool off. I stayed right there with the guys and we just battled the thing through – night and day – until we solved all our problems. When Dutton arrived back we're rolling to beat hell, putting more asphalt out than we ever did before."

The airport and highway paving jobs were coming in so fast, the boys simply couldn't find enough equipment to handle all the production that was required.

On one airport job at Claresholm, they could see there was no way to meet their deadline commitment unless they could find another paving machine.

Reg knew of a road-mix paving machine which had been developed and was owned by the provincial government. A huge, cumbersome thing, it was known as the "Queen Mary."

"We were really in trouble," Dutton said. "There was only one solution — Reg has to go up to Edmonton and get that goddamn machine from the government."

Paving Glenmore Trail

Norm McPherson was the Alberta Highway Commissioner at the time, and Reg knew him well. In a day or two, Reg returned with the machine. Just when it looked like they were going to make up some time, the rains came and threatened to shut everything down. There was no way oil and rain would mix together with the sand and gravel. It looked again like the deadline was beyond reach.

"To hell with it," said Reg, "we'll keep 'er running until we are forced to stop."

Meanwhile, the government inspectors maintained a constant vigil for anyone compromising specifications. Mixing and laying asphalt in the rain was considered absolutely unacceptable. The rain persisted, and eventually the young engineer from Ottawa made his appearance for a routine inspection. Luckily, Dutton got wind of his arrival and intercepted him before he got to the job site.

"I meet him and he wants to go right out and survey the airport. Reg has got everything shut down waiting until this engineer makes his inspection. I don't know what the hell to do with the guy, but we go out to the job and this guy is wading around in the puddles, examining all the rain-soaked materials and equipment."

"It's too wet – you can't proceed," the inspector said.

"Get that son-of-a-bitch out of here," Reg whispered in Dutton's ear.

Dutton knew the engineer enjoyed his booze, and he lured him back to the car with the promise of a snort or two of whiskey.

"I got one snort into him, and then another, and eventually I talked him into looking at another part of the project about three miles away. I no sooner get the car turned around and driving away when Reg got the men back to work and started up the machines. When I stopped the car, I can hear this machinery rumbling away in the distance," Dutton said.

"What the hell is that noise?" asked the engineer.

"Oh that's a train, comes by every day about this time. It's just over the hill there."

Eventually the inspector wanted to go downtown and get comfortable until his plane departed the following day. Once again Dutton played the role of the gracious host, and whisked the unsuspecting bureaucrat off to Calgary's finest watering holes and eateries.

Reg persevered until the job was completed, much of it under difficult, wet conditions.

"That was the first time we ever discovered you could actually mix oil and gravel with a little water," Reg said.

"It bound the gravel together better," said Dutton with a wink.

THE JENNINGS-DUTTON partnership flourished for two basic reasons. They admired each other, and each had the capacity to ignore the other during bouts of frustration. Dutton had a passion for big projects. Jennings had a vision well into the future, and a plan for getting there. Dutton's job was to ensure that the company always had opportunities to bid on the large construction projects which were coming up in Western Canada. Jennings made sure the bids were sound and profitable. His genius was management and organization, based on a grass-roots understanding of the business. It would be difficult to conceive two more opposite personalities. Dutton – big, aggressive and gruff; Jennings – small, gentle, but coldly methodical and innovative.

And while they indulged their passion for going after every major construction job that came along, an empire was growing up around them. It wasn't an empire they set out to build. The sheer pull of their leadership and energy attracted people to them and the empire grew.

When they began digging, leveling and grading the barren prairie that was to become the Calgary airport, Reg and Merv joined forces on a handshake. Dutton and his Dutton Brothers firm were the dirt movers. Jennings, with his Oliver machinery crew, leveled and surfaced the durable runways which were to become the foundation of one of Canada's busiest airports. They worked well together, and it was obvious to both of them that a more formal arrangement was needed to mold their separate teams into an integrated organization.

Standard Gravel and Surfacing Ltd. was formed in 1941 with the shrewd guidance of Harold Millican, Q.C., a pioneer Calgary lawyer and unrepentant Liberal organizer, fund-raiser and unsuccessful federal candidate.

"When we formed the company in 1941, we had three partners," Jennings said, "I took a third, Dutton Brothers took a third, and Bob Paget, with his Assiniboine Engineering firm, took a third." John Denholm, CA, recalled the precise terms of organization. On April 10, 1941, Standard Gravel & Surfacing Co. Ltd. was incorporated with nine shares in paid up capital, M. A. Dutton and Reginald F. Jennings with two shares each, and five other shareholders with one share each.

"As the work progressed, we bought all the shares from Paget, Jack Dutton and Fred Owens, a partner in Dutton Brothers."

"Owens was an old Mannix hand," Dutton recalled. "He was our bookkeeper — but what a man he was. He waged a running battle against engineers. He lived to fight because he figured everybody was trying to do him in."

"If you couldn't get along with the project engineer, you were in bad trouble. Reg had a facility for getting along with engineers; and so did I," said Dutton with a wink. "But not Owens — we had to buy him out to keep peace."

Eventually Reg and Merv emerged as the two major shareholders in Standard Gravel.

Between 1941 and 1945, Standard Gravel built about twenty airports all over Western Canada as part of the Commonwealth Air Training Plan. The clear skies over Western Canada's open prairie became the prep school for the allied combat fighters from Britain, Australia, New Zealand and Canada. The Commonwealth airmen served their basic training and acquired their flying skills at dozens of flying training schools in Western Canada. The newly trained pilots shipped out to war theatres all over the world. The Commonwealth Air Training Plan was the forerunner of the flying training programs for the North Atlantic Treaty Organization.

As Standard Gravel grew and flourished, another company, which became known as Burns and Dutton Construction, began to grow and take shape as a major building contractor.

Bob Burns, a gangly, gentle soul of six-foot-five, had grown up in Calgary as the son of a small concrete contractor. The steely-eyed discipline of Burn's father, gave him that intangible feel for the business, which in today's jargon is known as "technical expertise". Bob had been working on the maintenance crew at the Calgary Exhibition and Stampede Grounds.

It was the end of the first week in July 1941. The cowboys had moved on to the next rodeo, the midway was loaded on the train headed for Edmonton, and the smell of hot dogs and candy floss was beginning to dissipate into the atmosphere. It had been a busy week for big Bob, and he was looking forward to a few days off. Dutton and Jennings were busy trying to meet their time commitments in finishing the Woodcock Airport, south of Prince Rupert. They needed a concrete man to build the drains and storm sewers in order to complete the contract. Someone mentioned that big Bob Burns might be available. He was known to be a first class concrete man.

"I was suddenly under pressure to do my bit for the war effort, and before I knew it, Sandy Allison and I were on a train headed for an unknown destination called Woodcock," Burns said from his retirement home in the California desert south of Palm Springs. It turned out to be the most important decision of his life. In his casual but efficient manner, Burns handled his assignment with impressive skill and alacrity.

Dutton and Jennings saw opportunities all around them for concrete work and construction – curbs, gutters, sewer systems, warehouses and bridges.

A concrete company had been formed by Dutton before the outbreak of war in 1939 to give his sons Joe and Alex an opportunity to get started in business. The boys had joined the R.C.A.F., and were killed within six months of each other in missions over Germany. It was a tragic time for the Dutton family. The boys were survived by their mother, Phyllis, and a brother and sister, Norman and Beryl. Dutton bore the family bereavement quietly, but it was to remain with him forever.

As the need for concrete construction services became more obvious, Reg moved in with Bob Burns and Dutton to activate the concrete company. It was agreed that Dutton's remaining son, Norman, could have Dutton's shares.

Norman, however, had other plans. He had taken preliminary steps to join the Royal Canadian Air Force. Dutton was adamant.

"I didn't want him in the air force, that's for damn sure. I had lost the other two kids in the air force and I was damned if I was going to see Norman go the same way," Dutton said.

Dutton convinced Norman that he couldn't bear to see him in the air force, and then convinced air force officials to release him. But Norman was determined to join the forces and ended up in the navy. Norman served four years in the Royal Canadian Navy and returned home at war's end unscathed, but suffering the early symptoms of arthritis, which was to grow continually more painful and debilitating.

Meanwhile the Burns and Dutton Concrete and Construction Company began to flourish with Burns, Dutton and Jennings as equal partners.

"It started off as a little concrete company doing sidewalks, manholes and curbs," Jennings said. "Any concrete we had to do - especially on those airport jobs - we sublet to Burns and Dutton. It grew into a building company, taking on larger and larger contracts. The intent was to restrict Standard Gravel and Surfacing to roads, airports and dams, and allow Burns and Dutton to be the building arm of our organization," Jennings said.

Jubilee Auditorium, 1955 · *Glenbow Archives*

The first building contract undertaken by Burns and Dutton was a city fire hall at the corner of fourteenth street and thirtieth avenue south west in Calgary. It went from there to the Pacific Petroleums building on ninth avenue, and on to the two Jubilee Auditoriums in Calgary and Edmonton.

Burns was in charge, and he had an uncanny gift for the construction business. But he had an Achilles heel. Bob fell victim to an over-enthusiastic taste for whiskey. As the enterprise grew and flourished, Bob's alcohol intake increased, and he became increasingly less attentive to business, and would disappear for days on end. Burns depended too heavily on his highly-competent superintendent, Sid Staines, who maintained a firm hand on the jobs and kept things growing. But Burns' disappearances continued at an increasing rate. Reg and Merv were uneasy and were convinced something had to be done.

"You're going to have to fire him," Dutton told Reg one day.

"Fire him – you can't fire him – he's a partner," Reg replied.

Dutton decided to face Burns head on.

"I said: O.K. you son-of-a-bitch – it's either you or me – you could kill me. You're out or I'm out, and I'm not getting out."

Merv said the confrontation left the big man stunned and confused. Burns wandered off.

Later that very day he phoned Dutton.

"Merv, I've joined Alcoholics Anonymous and I'm coming back to work," Burns said.

"I didn't think the AA would take him – but by God, he hasn't taken a drink since that day and that was several years ago."

Eventually Burns and Dutton was re-organized and infused with new and enthusiastic partners, including Jack Simpson, a competent and hard driving construction hand.

Keith Matthews, a professional engineer recalled in a detailed summary the evolution of Burns and Dutton to become one of Canada's premier construction firms. In 1962, Burns, Simpson, H. R. Auck and H. A. Thomas acquired the company from Standard Holdings for a cash payment of $600,000 and an indebtedness of two million dollars. Along with the assets of the company, the new owners acquired work in progress of about ten million dollars. Jack Simpson, experienced and shrewd, joined the company with a vision for large building projects. The company was reorganized as Burns and Dutton Construction (1962) Ltd. Several schools, university buildings and commercial high rises were undertaken in a period of steady growth and prosperity. Bob Burns retired in 1968, and in 1970 the company became CANA Construction Company Ltd. with J. L. Simpson, President; H. Thomas, Vice President and H. R. Auck, Secretary-Treasurer. Taking on major projects across the country, CANA established branch offices in Edmonton, Saskatoon, Regina and other points as major projects emerged.

Back in 1927, when Reg was still in charge of the Commercial Cartage surfacing operation, he met a crusty Scotsman named John Boyd. On a joint venture with Boyd's General Construction Company from Vancouver, they laid the first pavement in Alberta from Calgary to Cochrane. At the same time, Marshall Paving in Edmonton paved a strip of highway between Ponoka and Lacombe in Central Alberta.

Born in 1887 in Hawick, Scotland, Boyd arrived in Canada penniless in 1906. He worked as a laborer in construction on the prairies, and moved to Victoria, where he got a job driving a team of horses.

In 1914, John Boyd became a partner in the A.B. Palmer Company, a construction firm. By this time he had acquired sound experience in railway and road construction work as well as general construction work.

General Construction Co. Limited was formed in 1924 as a subsidiary of A.B. Palmer Company for the purpose of carrying out all types of asphalt work. Asphalt technology was very much in its infancy in Western Canada. In 1926, on the retirement of A.B. Palmer, Boyd purchased both companies and carried on business under the name General Construction.

Reg Jennings and Jack Boyd maintained their friendship, with the result that Standard Gravel and General Construction shared a lot of major contracts on a joint venture basis, particularly in British Columbia.

Boyd's company joined forces with Dutton and Jennings and Jay McLaughlin in building the John Day Dam on the Columbia River and the Ice Harbor Dam in Southeastern Washington.

Jack Boyd retired from construction work in the early 1950s. The existing trend toward bigger and more complex construction projects, coupled with the Jennings-Dutton desire to conquer new fields, led to the merger of the two companies in 1963. The new company operated under the name Standard-General Construction (International), with Dutton as Chairman of the Board and Jennings as President and Chief Executive Officer of the new company. Standard-General now had a capacity to sponsor and operate major construction projects all across Western Canada and into the United States. And indeed it did.

In Reg Jennings' opinion "to be a good general contractor you have to have the guts and ingenuity to tackle any kind of a proposition, whether you know anything about it or not. We just went out and found the proper means to do the job."

President Bob Boon delivers
Christmas message, 1978

In this era of growth, the company, sometimes with joint venture partners, tackled an endless series of large-scale projects. The jobs included a floating bridge across Okanagan Lake at Kelowna, access roads and tunneling for a strip mine in the Queen Charlotte Islands (500 miles north of Vancouver), the Glenmore Causeway in Calgary; the Squaw Rapids Dam near Carrot River, Saskatchewan as well as the South Saskatchewan Dam, the Bonnington Dam near Nelson, British Columbia, the Boundary Dam near Metaline Falls, Washington; the Seymour Dam near Vancouver; the Alexandra Bridge across the Fraser River; the Fall Creek Dam near Eugene Oregon; the Yale Tunnel on the TransCanada Highway; the Tsawwassen Ferry Terminal near Vancouver; a major section of the Mid-Canada-Line (a defense and communications system across Canada's north); the S-shaped railway bridge and trestle across the Peace River at Taylor Flats,

British Columbia, rail-bed and bridges near the International Nickel mines in Northern Manitoba; twenty-seven airports and thousands of miles of highway in Western Canada. In addition to this the company built countless roadways, sewers and sidewalks in sub-division developments in Vancouver, Calgary, Edmonton and several other cities and towns in Western Canada.

"We had so goddamn many things going on, we couldn't keep track of it all," Dutton said. But as usual Jennings was keeping track of every detail and the company was showing handsome profits.

Boundary Dam, Washington State ·
Gary Baird, Boundary Dam Operations

It wasn't all construction either. Both Reg and Merv were open to new ideas and new opportunities. In 1948, the Calgary Stampeders Football team and its rabid followers invaded Toronto, where they were to meet and humiliate the Toronto Argos in the Grey Cup final. Both men were staunch supporters of the team both morally and financially.

Frank Kershaw, a football fan and a Winnipeg movie theatre operator, was motoring toward Toronto, across Wisconsin, Minnesota, Illinois and Michigan. A phenomenon began to unfold as he drove eastward. Huge movie screens were being erected in large parking lots, and were called Drive-In Theatres. Kershaw was excited with the new idea, and began a process of conjecture as to how and where this idea could be applied in Canada.

In Toronto, he met Dutton and Jennings celebrating the Calgary Grey Cup triumph in their suite at the Royal York Hotel. He couldn't resist trying the idea out on the two Calgary entrepreneurs.

"Go get us some information," they instructed him, "and we'll take a look at it."

A man who knew a good idea and business opportunity when he saw one, Kershaw persisted, and a short time later, showed up in Calgary armed with more information. Reg and Merv followed this up with a trip to the U.S., where they saw drive-ins springing up like mushrooms, with long lineups of cars passing by the box office. It was an all-cash business with plenty of volume. They decided to take the plunge. A company was formed in late 1948, with Dutton, Jennings, Harold Millican, Ross Henderson and Kershaw, with Kershaw named Managing Director. Within weeks, they began construction of the Chinook Drive-In Theatre on the site that is now occupied by the Chinook Shopping Centre in southwest Calgary.

In 1950, Lightweight Aggregates of Canada was formed to manufacture and market an expanded, lightweight aggregate to replace sand and gravel in the manufacture of concrete blocks.

In September 1950, Canadian Pipe Line Construction was formed to build pipelines in any locality where opportunities arose in Canada. A principal in this company was Bill Bennett, the former deputy minister for C.D. Howe during the war. Others included: Jennings, Dutton, Jay McLaughlin and O.W. McIntyre of Great Falls, Montana.

In 1952, Don MacKay, a former mayor of Calgary, had an opportunity to acquire a General Motors franchise, but he didn't have the wherewithal to get established. Merv and Reg suggested that Merv's son, Norman, should go into partnership with MacKay and operate the business, and on that condition, agreed to support the idea. Stampede Motors Ltd. was incorporated with the four partners as principals.

About that same time, Reg and Ed Jefferies began talking about the efficiencies of a merger between the light-weight aggregate plant and the Jefferies' block plant. Working on another level were Chick Thorssen and Ross Jefferies, who were close personal friends. Thorssen was deeply involved in the development process. The talks resulted in a merger into a company known as Consolidated Concrete Industries. B.A. Monkman, a concrete expert, was appointed Operating Head of the company.

By 1953, there were thirty-five companies under the control of Dutton and Jennings.

"Merv and I worried a lot about it," Jennings said. "We were flying all over the country in all directions, and if anything had ever happened to either one of us, it was so goddamn complicated, nobody would ever sort it out."

Jennings and Dutton wanted to accomplish two things. They wanted to get their personal estates into manageable order, and they wanted to transfer shares in the company to the key employees.

Fairview Redimix Plant

The original idea was to form another company which would be used to distribute shares to the employees. Harold Millican, legal advisor, suggested they go to Ottawa and incorporate the new company under a Federal Charter. Jennings and Dutton insisted that the new federal company retain the name Standard Gravel and Surfacing. This posed some difficulty, because a Standard Construction Company in Toronto held a Federal Charter and two federal companies could not have the same name.

The Undersecretary of State, Mr. O'Meara, advised Millican the company name could be preserved by simply adding the words "of Canada Limited" at the end. The partners were delighted, and returned to Calgary where they would proceed with distributing shares in the company to certain key employees.

Reg and Merv took preferred stock in the new company as their share of Standard Gravel and Surfacing Ltd. The common shares of the new company were all distributed to the key employees and to the immediate heirs of Reg and Merv. It was one of the most magnanimous gestures ever witnessed in Canadian business circles. A company with an estimated $50 million in assets was sold to the employees for $1,600,000.

The distribution of shares had been accomplished, but the structure of the company was still not adequate to accommodate the Dutton-Jennings share ownership in all of the various other companies in which they had an interest. It was so complex that the best legal advice they could get in Calgary was to go to Toronto and contact the Palmer law firm, which had a reputation for this kind of work. Palmer had performed legal work for C.D. Howe during the war years. He assigned an expert corporate and tax lawyer to the case, a man called Creber.

Creber put together Standard Holdings Ltd. with Reg and Merv as sole owners. All of their interests in more than thirty-five companies were sold to this company for some cash, but mainly redeemable preferred shares. As the various companies paid dividends, Reg and Merv used the cash to redeem the shares.

"Those Palmer lawyers did a helluva good job for us," Reg said. "When BACM came along to buy us out, we simply sold them Standard Holdings."

Dutton & Jennings:
the Standard Saga

❖

DAILY ROUTINE FOR A CONSTRUCTION BOSS ranges from day and night supervision and vigilance on remote job sites to complex negotiations in mahogany boardrooms. On a given day, he and the crew might be fighting hordes of mosquitoes at a job site in the northern muskeg, and days later be huddled in a corporate boardroom in tense negotiations with the nation's industrial and financial captains.

Jennings and Dutton were at home in either atmosphere.

"Weather conditions could be your friend or enemy," Jennings said.

"One year when the TransCanada Highway first started, the weather hung tough against us all summer. We had a section to pave from Cluny to Strathmore, and we completed the grand total of one and a half-miles during the whole summer. We should have completed the whole job – but it wouldn't stop raining.

"We were really scratching that winter. We had to keep the men going, overhaul the machinery, and keep the shop running. I was really sleeping with the banker that winter," Reg said.

"Everytime the bank manager saw Reg, he put the stethoscope on him," Dutton said. "There's no gamble in the world like contracting. They're pikers in Las Vegas."

Construction men have ways to protect themselves in the estimating process. They take soil tests, test the quality and availability of gravel, material and personnel. But the weather is always uncertain, and often, there will be unexpected conditions to face.

One of the most frustrating jobs of Dutton's recollection was the Mackenzie Highway job from Grimshaw to the Northwest Territories, miles of highway through bush, muskeg and boulders. It was a joint venture with Manor Construction, with Standard the sponsor and facing a contractor's most peculiar nemesis: permafrost. And that was in mid-July.

Permafrost is a phenomenon that can be described as an intricate network of glass-like ice shards frozen in place underlying the surface of northern terrain. Northern muskeg is like a huge frozen sponge. When the earth's surface is disturbed, the icy sub-structure begins to melt and turns the entire area into a quagmire. It is therefore necessary in road building through muskeg to remove the unstable overburden to a depth where there is a solid base, and replace it with stable material.

Chapter Eight:
The Jobs

"The contract called for building the road from Grimshaw to Hay River for $2 million, which we did, but there wasn't much left over when we were through," Jennings said.

Mackenzie Highway winter work from Keg River to Hay River, 1959

Reg and Merv were present in the camps most of the time, working with the men, supervising, and for the most part searching for economic methods to stabilize the roadbed.

"There was one tangent, eighty-five miles as straight as a goose flying south, and parallel to it was choice dirt for fill, but the government wouldn't allow us to use it," Dutton recalled.

Government specification insisted that it was important that the terrain be subjected to a minimum of scarring.

"Finally we got the engineer up there, and I showed him how we were forced to haul dirt for several miles to use as fill. We had seven cats pushing and thirteen dirt movers hauling more than three quarters of a mile . . . and boulders the size of an easy chair . . . that's what we built that goddamn road out of."

Mackenzie Highway

"You could get lost in that wilderness if you wandered off the right-of-way, and the mosquitoes were twice as big as that (indicating half a thumb). We used $3,400 worth of mosquito oil on the job."

The mosquitoes were apparently attracted by the odor of diesel fuel used in the heavy equipment. A large barrel of mosquito oil had been placed by the door of the cook shack, available to the men as they returned to work from their meals. The workmen literally doused their heads and faces with the oil about three times each day.

The raw, rustic beauty of the terrain made a permanent impression on both Reg and Merv.

"I told Herb McLaughlin one day," Merv said, "there must be something in this country besides bush and blue skies."

"I always carried a 'mickey' with me," Merv recalled. "It was getting toward noon time, and I had discovered a spring that bubbled pure, ice cold water. Reg took off up to the spring with a thermos bottle . . . we wanted a little touch of whiskey and water before lunch. Reg was gone about ten minutes, and he came back absolutely crawling with mosquitoes . . . I never saw anything like it in my life . . . my skin got so tough the mosquitoes couldn't get through it."

Conditions in the camp were typical of the period. There were no movies or television or other forms of entertainment. The men ate, slept and worked. There were two or three battery radios, but reception was so poor it was more aggravation than pleasure.

Camp food was outstanding in keeping with the tradition to feed construction men the very best available while in camp.

"The men were given three and four course meals, and they could have almost anything they wanted including steaks, chicken, fresh vegetables and a variety of home-made desserts," Dutton recalled.

Every third or fourth day, the entire camp was uprooted and moved along the highway right-of-way on rubber-tired flat beds. It was important to have the shacks and sleeping quarters close to where the work was being done.

The railway went as far north as Notikewin, which is 368 miles north of Edmonton. From there on north was a fading tractor trail that had once been used by the U.S. Army during the war years.

The work continued on into the fall and winter. The thermometer dipped to 72 below Fahrenheit for one period, and the men were instructed to leave the equipment running constantly because it was too cold to start in the morning.

During this cold snap, a portable repair shop caught fire and burned to the ground.

Reg and Merv made the trip up to the location by car, with an insurance adjuster in tow.

"We made sure he kept warm. All the way up and all the way back we poured rum into him," Dutton said. "On the way back, it was snowing and it was like driving into a solid white wall. The only way we could tell if we were off the road was if the wheel fell into the ditch. We would back it up and move over."

The Mackenzie Highway job was completed in just under two years, and the $2 million price tag didn't provide for an excess of profit. It served as a valuable lesson in the estimating process. The Mackenzie job was one of the last jobs completed that didn't include asphalt surfacing.

One of the next major challenges was the Banff-Jasper Highway. It was a ribbon of highway hacked, blasted and chiseled through one of the most majestic mountain ranges in the world. The contract, let by the Federal Department of Mines and Resources, continued for almost four years until completion.

It was not unusual for contractors to form partnerships combining personnel and equipment when bidding major jobs. Gerry Stotts, an engineer with J. A. Moulson Construction Ltd. in the late 1950s, recalled his firm teaming up with Standard to tackle road building and earth moving projects throughout Alberta.

A total of eleven highway grading contracts were completed on Highway 2, Calgary-Edmonton; Banff-Jasper; TransCanada; Yellowhead and Mackenzie Highway.

Equipment from both companies was used on each contract. The job sponsor was selected to supervise the project, and the resulting profit was shared by the partners based on the equipment rentals charged to the project.

The Banff-Windermere, another road through the scenic wilderness was slashed up the seven miles to Storm Mountain, across a high pass, across the Great Divide into British Columbia and along the Kootenay River.

"The road across Storm Mountain was a dirty, miserable piece of highway to build," Jennings remembered. "It was all silt and slide scree and basic muck. It was absolutely muck . . . the men called it 'loonshit.' It all had to be taken out and replaced with a stable fill before you could start with anything that looked like a road."

Certain of the hundreds of jobs tackled in all kinds of conditions over a period of more than thirty years seem to linger more vividly in Reg's memory. The Banff-Windermere was one of them.

"The chief engineer, a French-Canadian named Claude, from the federal department came out from Ottawa to inspect the work and negotiate some prices for the contract.

Banff-Jasper Highway, Caterpillar D8 and 435 Pull Scraper, 1963

"The poor guy landed on a late flight into Calgary where Dutton and I met him. Claude was exhausted and wanted to go to bed, but there was no way Dutton would let him get to bed until we completed the negotiations. And all the while he was pouring drinks into him.

"We kept at it until five o'clock in the morning . . . we wore the poor bastard out . . . he was so tired, he would gladly have given us the highway. I was getting so goddamn tired I couldn't stay awake, and I told Dutton to lay off poor old Claude and give him some rest. No sir, he was going to finish negotiations come hell or high water."

Reg explained that most of the highway jobs were priced out on a unit basis. The contractor gets a certain fee per cubic yard for all 'cull and excavation'. Added to this is another agreed upon price per cubic yard for crushing and screening the gravel, another fee per cubic yard for hauling the gravel. Spreading and rolling brought another fee, and of course, the asphalt manufacture and laying down was charged out separately.

Negotiations involved a debate between the contractor and the government engineer as to what could be agreed upon as a fair price for each of the various steps in the process.

It became apparent to Claude that the details of the contract must be ironed out if he was ever going to get any rest. He finally knuckled under to Dutton's relentless pressure, and toddled off to bed.

When the Banff-Windermere was completed to Radium, Standard built the tunnel through Sinclair Canyon as well as the bath house facilities at Radium.

Dutton described the tunnel burrowing under the bath house and the swimming pools as the "tunnel of love." The entire facility at Radium was a Standard-Gravel contract, but it was farmed out to Burns and Dutton Construction.

Reg explained that Standard was involved in the construction of every mile of highway from the Saskatchewan border to the British Columbia border. "At various times over the years we worked various portions and performed several different types of construction on every mile of road from the U.S. border to the Northwest Territories and beyond," Jennings said. "And we did the south-provincial highway from Walsh, Medicine Hat, Lethbridge and up through Blairmore, through Crows Nest Pass to the British Columbia border. Either we graded or we paved, or we graveled or we'd build a bridge or did some damn thing."

Intense rivalry existed between the two major operating companies — Standard Gravel and Burns and Dutton Construction. Key personnel in both organizations were largely hard-working, strong-minded men and personalities in the two organizations were constantly colliding head-on. Reg believes that the people in each of the organizations firmly believed they could do construction better than the other. Ironically, Standard directed its attention exclusively to road and airport building, while Burns and Dutton concentrated on buildings.

There was one minor exception, when Standard was given the job of building a road to the top of Sulphur Mountain. The federal government wanted a meteorogical station on top of the mountain, but first a road had to be built.

"We didn't bother to have Burns and Dutton build that station . . . it was part of the same contract, and we had to take the supplies in anyway," Reg said.

Sinclair Canyon, Windermere Highway ·
Glenbow Archives

Frequently in the geneology of the Dutton-Jennings group of companies would appear the name of a hitherto unheard of construction company. It was usually a major job in a remote area that inspired these new organizations to emerge. These companies were organized for a reason, sometimes financial, sometimes geographical, and almost always to take advantage of the provisions in the tax regime of the period.

One such company was Aklavik Construction Ltd., which listed its management as Vince Dunne, President; John Denholm, Vice-President and Treasurer; and Pat Mahoney, Secretary.

Aklavik took on contracts in the Northwest Territories, one of which was the Norman Wells Airport on the Mackenzie River. The Norman Wells job was described in the June, 1961 issue of Standard Screenings, the publication of the Standard group of companies.

"Bob Scott reports that everything is going well in the far north. The starting date on the runway was June 6, and by June 18, 75,000 cubic yards of dirt were excavated with three DW-21s and two push cats. While the equipment is working on the main runway, airlines are using a temporary strip adjacent to it. Grading was completed on the parking apron June 18th, and the placing of four inches of gravel is now underway."

"The completion date of the first work is estimated at August 15th, at which time the three DW-21s and one push cat will be sent to Blackie Paron's job on the Mackenzie Highway. These will be shipped by barge to Hay River."

In the early part of April, Dutton and Jennings asked Bob Scott when the first barges would arrive at Norman Wells with the dirt moving equipment.

He replied "June 1st", and as predicted, they docked on June 1st. "You can check our last bulletin to verify his statement," Reg recalled. Even the tug-boat captain was amazed at Bob's fearless prediction.

The start of the project on June 6th was highlighted by the arrival of two representatives of the Department of Transport. These were: G.W. Smith, Chief Engineer, Airport Development, Ottawa, and V.R. Currie, Regional Construction Engineer, Edmonton.

Scott's report added: "Gus Gustafson and Roger Blais who are operating the crusher have put through 5,000 tons of 3", which will be used on the drainage. Conditions encountered in the north are often baffling, and one such is the frost in the gravel stockpiled last winter during very low temperatures. Gus Gustafson estimates the present temperature of this gravel at 10 below zero a few feet below the surface. When it is dumped into the trap at the crusher, it immediately freezes to the walls and will not flow to the conveyor belt.

"However, the project superintendent, H. Jensen, with the help of the crusher crew, a few pieces of iron, a small motor and part of a vibratory compactor, solved the problem.

This Rube Goldberg invention creates a violent vibration which prevents material from freezing to the metal.

"The cook house chief has 13 men on his staff. This sounds like a lot of cooks, but they have many varied duties, such as washing dishes, cutting meat, cleaning all the bunkhouses, washrooms, kitchens and diners, and looking after the warehouse, the coolers and freezers. Since all operations are on a double shift basis, four meals are served daily with two sittings at breakfast and dinner.

"In one of the pictures you will notice a quonset hut. This is the storehouse for non-perishable food, and the present stock adds up over 40 tons. This is necessary because of the long distance from the source of supply. Last week the camp steward was worried because his meat reserve was down to 3,000 pounds.

"Fastball is the favorite pastime, with Aklavik Constructors battling members of D.O.T. The games are played on the airfield and the umpire never has to call a game on account of darkness. The sun sets at approximately 11:00 p.m. A very lively recreation committee has made it possible for the boys to see two movies a week. There are no television sets in Norman Wells.

"We must congratulate all employees on this project on their safety record. Since the start of the project last September there has been only one lost time accident. Considering the number of hours worked, and a good percentage of those in extreme temperatures with no daylight, we feel that the boys have done very well."

And so it was with the Norman Wells Airport.

Frequently, the jobs called for skills and technical expertise which had to be brought in, or if it was unavailable, improvisation took place on the job site.

In the early 1960s, Calgary's traffic began to choke the few arteries linking the downtown with the rapidly-growing south side. The city fathers decided the artificial lake created by the Glenmore Dam on the Elbow River should be spanned by a causeway allowing a further traffic artery to cope with the mounting traffic jams.

Hundreds of hours planning and studies plus exhaustive hydraulic tests went into the design and specifications of the Glenmore Causeway.

Arnold Berg, Standard Gravel's Project Superintendent, said the most troublesome part of the job was done before the project really began.

"There was a terrific amount of preliminary work," Berg claims.

The record bears him out. Before the job began, 13,000 feet of snowfence were installed on both sides of the access road to prevent accidents to children living in the area.

The access road was then graded, graveled and oiled from the Glenmore project site to the city-owned gravel pit, a distance of three-and-a-half miles. Then 250,000 cubic yards of dirt were removed from the Glenmore area as a preliminary road grading measure.

The Miller 600 Extruder, 1972

Some of this dirt was hauled to a coulee north of the filtration plant to build a grade for an extension on 16th Street coming south from 50th Avenue. The rest was moved one-and-a-half miles to strengthen the dike along the southeast side of the reservoir.

Three big screening plants were moved to the gravel pit site especially for the Causeway project. Because a gas line ran through the middle of the gravel pit, it became necessary to remove gravel from a narrow thirty-foot trench at the edge of the site. A new gas line was then laid in this trench, the old pipe removed and work was able to proceed.

A further problem arose over getting fill from the west to the east side of the reservoir.

The only access was over a narrow bridge at the dam site. Since a constant stream of supply trucks across this bridge would have caused grave inconvenience to the public, Standard Gravel constructed a temporary gravel fill road across the new bridge channel.

A fifty-four-inch culvert was then installed beneath the crossing to handle the water flow between the two sides of the reservoir. With the completion of the bridge, this culvert was removed.

In order to facilitate work on the causeway, the city arranged to lower the regular water level of the Glenmore Reservoir by fourteen feet. However, divers still had to work under some 28 feet of water.

A check with several major construction firms in Western Canada and the United States reveals that individual placement of rip-rap on underwater projects of this kind is probably unique in North America.

The use of selected material (3/4 ton rip-rap) is also unusual. Rip-rap is the term used to describe the placement of huge boulders as stabilizers in construction projects.

One of the first problems facing Standard Gravel was where to find the experienced men to do the job.

They were fortunate in obtaining the services of Universal Diving Ltd., of Vancouver. Their experienced eight-man crew put in twenty-hour days on the Glenmore project. Each of the four divers worked along in two-and-a-half-hour shifts, in almost complete underwater darkness. Maximum visibility was one foot, usually the diver was lucky to be able to see a few inches ahead. Thus placement of the rip-rap had to be done completely be feel, under telephoned instructions from the diver.

On the barge, tenders were busy too. They had to make sure that communication was retained between the diver and the crane operator, ensure that no rock load was swung over the diver's bubbles, direct the diver to the site and stand by to rescue him in case of accident.

Divers were Al Black, who learned diving techniques during a wartime navy stint, George Hazleton, Ralph Somerville and Al Trice, each of whom had at least nine years diving experience.

There was a high rate of flow in the reservoir and a loose silt bottom. The decision to rip-rap was the result of exhaustive hydraulic model studies. The job, of course, demanded pinpoint precision. To assure greater precision, superintendent Pat Naughton designed a giant ten foot wrap-around protractor.

Glenmore Causeway · *Glenbow Archives*

An 80-D Northwest Crane was accurately spotted by means of line and grade stakes, and the protractor was mounted on the front of the crane. The rock was lowered by grapple. The diver instructed the crane operator by telephone, and surface men kept a lifeline on the man below. The protractor determined the sweep within the perimeter of the channel apron. A boom indicator determined the boom angle. Swing angle readings were accurate to the nearest degree. Angles at which the line of operations would cross the channel were carefully plotted and graphed before work started. The job foreman, working from the divers' scow, plotted actual progress of rip-rap placement on a planned view.

Winter weather set in by early December, and it began to look as if the job at the new Glenmore Causeway would be shut down for several months by ice formation in the reservoir.

The problem was solved when Standard Gravel brought in a 600-cubic-foot compressor which was attached to a submerged hose, weighted with half-inch cable. The hose had holes its entire length. Compressed air escaping through these holes agitated the water sufficiently to prevent freezing in the channel work area.

For a few days in December, when the weather dropped to about twenty below zero, it was necessary to use two hoses. For the rest of the time, one hose sufficed. Underwater placement of the rip-rap was completed before Christmas. The job was completed on time and on budget, and today the Glenmore Causeway still provides one of the major traffic arteries between south Calgary and the downtown and northwest sector of the city.

It WASN'T LONG AFTER THE DUTTON-JENNINGS partnership in Standard Gravel was formed that they had so many jobs in so many widespread locations that it became difficult to get around to them all.

Both Reg and Merv felt it was important to make periodic visits to the job sites, and maintain good communication with the men on the job.

It was inevitable that they should buy an aircraft, and before they were finished they had an entire fleet of them. Flying was to provide some of the zaniest and most exciting moments of their high tension construction life.

Their first aircraft was a Cessna Trainer. It had been in mothballs in Medicine Hat and still had the original Royal Canadian Air Force yellow paint and markings. It had been used in the war time flying training program. All things considered, many years later Reg still believed it was worth the $5,000 they paid for it.

Their very first flight was an adventure.

"We had a pilot named Jim MacQueen who had been a pilot during the war. He had an old two-bit compass and we took off for Grande Prairie. None of us knew how in hell to get to Grande Prairie, but the fellow in the tower who cleared us said the Mannix plane was taking off just ahead, and we could follow him right into Grande Prairie."

On that occasion Fred Mannix was traveling with Harry Anderson, who was Chief Engineer for Highways for the Province of British Columbia.

"The Mannix plane had a little rinky-dink radio set-up which could make radio contact with Grande Prairie in case of trouble," Reg recalled. "The tower cleared us to go, and we were doing fine until about half way . . . just around Whitecourt we hit the goddamndest rain storm I ever saw. Dutton was in front with the pilot, and I was behind.

"We lost Mannix, we didn't know where the hell we were. All we did was follow that compass and we were losing altitude. When we finally came down out of the storm we were sitting on top of the trees . . . trees to the horizon in every direction.

"We had just about kissed ourselves goodbye when we came out of it, and there was a spot a way over on the horizon. It had just been a local storm, and the Mannix plane was returning to look for us.

Chapter Nine:
The Flyers

"We flew wing tip to wing tip all the way to Grande Prairie," said Reg. The plane arrived safely at about 10 a.m. Someone greeted them with a bottle of Black and White Scotch.

"We drank the whole goddamned bottle as soon as we got on the ground," said Reg.

"I was never so glad to get on the ground in my life," said Merv.

But that wasn't to be the end of the adventure on this particular junket. When they had finished their business in Grande Prairie, they ventured further north to visit job sites on the Grimshaw Highway, which Standard was building at the time.

Reg and Merv took off with MacQueen in the Cessna to Peace River and drove up the highway from there. On the return trip, they boarded the Cessna in Peace River for the return flight to Edmonton. Reg began a lookout for Lesser Slave Lake.

"We had been flying for about three quarters of an hour and I said to MacQueen: 'Where in the hell are you?'" Reg recalled.

MacQueen looked at the map and pointed to the location according to his calculation.

"If we are here, what the hell happened to Lesser Slave Lake?" asked Reg.

Dutton was in the front seat with the pilot and Reg was in the back with a sub-contractor who had hitched a ride.

"I can't remember his name," said Reg, "but he was one scared partridge."

Reg then instructed the pilot to turn right which would turn them in a more westerly direction.

"I'll be goddamned if he didn't and the first thing we saw was a bridge and the railway tracks. We followed that railroad all the way to Edmonton."

When that trip was safely completed, Reg and Merv re-assessed their air transportation program. They formulated a two-part plan. They decided to buy a better, larger plane and they decided to seek the advice of the legendary Punch Dickens, a well known Canadian bush pilot who was at this time involved in aircraft sales and rebuilding in Toronto.

Dickens sold the boys an Avro Anson. It was a two engine light bomber trainer that had been built at Fort William during the war.

"We put everything on that one," said Dutton. "Every flying instrument you could think of was on that plane."

❖

Above: deHavilland Dove
Left: Roy Jennings

❖

One of the most dramatic incidents connected with the Dutton-Jennings air exploits involved royalty and a brush with tragedy.

A subsidiary company under the direction of Jack Simpson, a construction superintendent who began his illustrious construction career with Standard, was performing work for the Eldorado Mining Company at Radium on Great Slave Lake. Aklavik Constructors, a Standard subsidiary, was rebuilding the crusher and the mill after a devastating fire at the site.

It was during the early period of uranium exploration and development, and the mine and crusher had attracted the attention of Prince Phillip, who was on one of his periodic visits to Canada with the Queen.

A tour and reception was arranged for Radium, and the dignitaries, in addition to Prince Phillip, included Bill Bennett, President of Eldorado Mining and Chairman of the Atomic Energy Commission; Frank Broderick, President of Northern Transportation; Reg, Merv and several members of their respective families including Reg's son Roy Jennings.

The Standard Gravel pilot again was Jim MacQueen. Reg had given him instructions and the method by which he should approach Radium.

Bennett had gone on ahead in the Eldorado DC-3, and had asked Reg if his wife could make the trip in the Standard plane, which was a deHavilland Dove. Mrs. Broderick, her son Paul, Roy Jennings and his brother-in-law Arnold Berg were also on the flight. Reg had explained to pilot Jim Lougheed there was a nice, easy waterway he could follow right into Sawmill Bay which is where he was to land on the approach to the mine. Lougheed seemed to understand and he took off with the excited passenger roster from Yellowknife.

"I had a premonition when he took off," said Reg. "He started off in the wrong direction . . . and I said, goddamn that guy has gone wrong."

Roy Jennings wrote the story entitled *The Flight of the Lonesome Dove*, printed below, which describes in frightening detail the adventure they were about to face.

"There was nothing unusual about August 8th, 1954. Just another sunny summer day, in the Northwest Territories, you might say. We were young, ambitious and excited about the promised growth and prosperity of the early fifties. But mostly, we worked hard and took our day-to-day jobs very seriously.

"Today though, was a treat. My father, Reg Jennings, had flown into Yellowknife on the company plane, and suggested myself and a colleague take a break.

"'Roy, why don't you and Arnold take that trip to Saw Mill Bay, the scenery up here is spectacular, and you boys deserve a day off!'

"We made our way to the Yellowknife airport, without a care in the world! We thought nothing of climbing aboard the aircraft 'deHavilland Dove' – which was destined for Saw Mill Bay, an easy two and a half-hour flight. The bright red and white twin engine executive aircraft belonged to Standard Gravel and Surfacing of Canada Limited. It was polished up, motor humming and ready to fly.

"Jim Lougheed was our pilot, an over-confident man who had taken this trip two or three times before. His co-pilot was Bob Millot.

"The passenger list was small, but impressive, and a group I'm sure I'll never forget. Betty Bennett and her son Paul were on their way up to meet up with her husband Bill, who was President of Atomic Energy of Canada. Frank Broderick, head of Northern Transportation Company, would be waiting for his wife Rosemary, who was also on the 'Dove'. The ladies were catching a floatplane from Saw Mill Bay, which would take them to Port Radium where the Duke of Edinburgh was to pay a visit during his tour of the Northwest Territories. Arnold Berg, Superintendent for Standard Gravel and Surfacing Limited, and myself, Roy Jennings, timekeeper for the same company rounded out the list of souls on board the deHavilland Dove.

"The aircraft flew down the runway and joined the birds, soaring high above the ground – all objects becoming smaller and almost disappearing from view. Arnold was staring out the window, his nose pressed against the glass.

"'That's Snare River Power, isn't that east of Yellowknife?' Arnold asked to no one in particular. Of course it was east of Yellowknife, and what's more is that we were flying east of the power plant. We were about five minutes into the flight and Arnold suspected we were off course.

"Bob, the co-pilot reached down and pulled open a map, apparently searching for a landmark. But our pilot was quick to react.

"'Put it away Bob, I've taken this trip before – I know exactly where I'm going.'

"Well two and half-hours came and went; idle conversation, the odd joke and family story passed the time. By now, Great Bear Lake should have been in view, but all we could see was tundra. We were flying due north looking for the south shore of Great Bear Lake. What seemed like an eternity passed, and finally a patch of blue was visible on the horizon. There was a collective sigh in the aircraft, as we all assumed this was the lake. Jim steered the aircraft westward and a little north. The landing strip at the settlement of Norman Wells oil refinery would soon be in sight.

"Norman Wells, however, did not come into our view, and we flew on, and on and on. In the distance, tiny white peaks could be seen in the water near the shore – they were icebergs! After hours of 'knowing exactly where he was going' Jim finally admitted that he was lost. Radio messages were sent to anyone out there that might hear us.

"There was a deafening silence in the plane. No response to our desperate call for help. There was static over the radio, and Jim's not-so confident voice pleaded for help. (We later discovered that all kinds of planes and stations in the Northwest Territories could hear us, but we were deaf, probably due to the magnetic pole.)

"We headed east, and after a short time, and to the relief of everyone on board a voice came over the radio. It was Max Ward, a famous bush pilot who was taking the Minister of Northern Affairs, John Lesage, into Coppermine for a visit to meet the Duke of Edinburgh.

"'I read you loud and clear Dove, describe the terrain.'

"Jim did so, saying we were on the south shore of Great Bear Lake.

"'Ice-bergs! That's most certainly NOT Great Bear Lake. I'm afraid you folks have made your way up to the Arctic Ocean! Bathurst Inlet is just east and an emergency landing would be next to impossible – it would probably have to be in the water. My recommendation is get headed west and try to reach the settlement of Coppermine on the mouth of Coppermine

River. Now, there is no landing strip there, pontoons are the only thing that flies in, so you'll have to make a forced landing somewhere in the area. Good luck!'

"Despite the fact we had Coppermine on the radio, and they were sending the RCMP, a Hudson's Bay agent and some of the local Eskimos out to check the stability of the sandbar, we knew that it was getting desperate. From our birds-eye vantage we could see the group sinking into the sand bar. They were in up to their knees. No one had to say it, we all knew – this was not the place for a forced landing.

"We had been in the air for over 6 hours. Jim finally said out loud what we all knew was happening, there was no fuel left. We would be out at any time. He flew south down Coppermine River and 18 miles down spotted a large sand bar in the middle of the river.

"'This is it, folks, there are no other options. Now, Roy and Bob, you guys get to the rear of the craft and open the back door and sit on the floor. We need as much weight as possible back there so the nose wheel of the tricycle landing gear won't hit the ground first.'

"Why couldn't I be 6'4", 270 pounds, I thought to myself as Bob and I headed to the back of the plane. You don't need a physics degree to imagine what would happen to the craft if the nose did touch first – the plane would be thrown into a ground loop, and the passengers would be killed or, at the very least, seriously injured.

"On approach, the starboard engine sputtered and died, it was amazing we had the fuel to get us that far! We were heading in at about 150 miles an hour. The Dove sailed and shimmied, catching each wind current, tossing the plane to and fro. As the plane dropped lower and lower, the landscaped flew past us, everything was a blur. The wind was rushing through the aircraft and I held my breath, praying we would make it safely down.

"Finally we came to a stop within three to four hundred feet. The thick sand slowed the wheels and our plane finally came to rest; its wheels buried in 6 to 8 inches of sand. Seconds after we landed the port engine ran out of fuel.

"At last, we were on God's green earth again. We piled out of the plane and threw ourselves on the ground, kissing the sand and giving thanks that we were all in one piece. There wasn't much to be said, so the pilot reached inside the plane and pulled out the scotch, vodka and dark rum which was stored behind the back seat. He set up an impromptu bar on the wing and proceeded to serve us up, finishing every drop that was on board while we awaited rescue.

"Because power was out after the landing there was no radio contact with Coppermine. But soon the RCMP and some Eskimos came to our rescue in boats loaded with blankets, and a fire extinguisher, which they thankfully did not have to use. They were almost as happy as we were to see that the landing was a success.

"We were taken to Coppermine by boat and arrangements were made for us to catch a floatplane to Port Radium. A 'Norseman' with Alf Kaywood, Chief Pilot of Eldorado Mining and Refining Company at the helm, transported the same passenger list.

"After our most memorable 'day off' ever, Arnold and myself went back to Yellowknife with Jim and Bob. We later discovered that our instincts were correct, the plane needed to land exactly as it did, or else it could have made a ground loop, killing everyone on board. We also learned that the pilot had one option, and that was to make a belly landing on the sandbar avoiding any chance of a ground loop. Of course, inquiries were made, and the company released Jim Lougheed. Incidentally the 'Dove' was not insured for the Northwest Territories, so not only were we lucky to have our lives, but the company was relieved to have the plane in one piece."

Meanwhile, Reg, Merv and the guests had arrived at the mine and were frantic with concern for the passengers in the other airplane.

"But here's Bennett sitting over at Radium," said Reg, "getting an erratic flow of signals from the plane, and the conversation between Ward and the pilot, and he is convinced the passengers have perished in the mouth of the Coppermine."

As it turned out a Norseman with floats was rushed into the sand bar and removed the passengers to safety at Radium where they were re-united with the group.

"In the meantime," said Reg, "Prince Phillip was on the way in, but our adventure stole the show for him."

Fortunately the luck of the "Dove" changed, at least temporarily. Unaccountably, someone had cached two barrels of aviation gas on the sand bar. With the help of some incredulous natives, they were able to wrestle planks under the wheels. When all was in readiness, Lougheed and his co-pilot revved the motor to maximum pitch and lifted the airplane off the sand bar.

They still had to face Reg in Yellowknife, who was embarrassed, outraged and impatient with people who couldn't keep their operation under control. Reg had a particular intolerance for wayward pilots.

While the lost plane was finding its way back to Yellowknife, Prince Phillip had come and gone in the shadow of public interest over the misadventure, while the Brodericks and the Bennetts had returned to the south in the Eldorado DC-3.

Unfortunately, Reg was to suffer even more discomfort at the hands of his hired pilots.

"On the way from Yellowknife to Uranium City, I was sitting behind the co-pilot with a map and I had a pretty good reading on the ground locations."

Reg had instructed the pilots to fly visually, follow the route and forget about "homing in on the goddamn Uranium City control station."

"By God, we got over Fort Smith and he had no idea where in hell he was."

They eventually got back on track, landed at Uranium City, and the following day flew all the way back to Calgary.

"Their pay stopped the following day," said Reg referring to his final dealings with the pilots.

The Uranium City job was only one of many that Aklavik Constructors performed in the north, and characteristically the innovative mind of Reg along with the hard-driving Jack Simpson, created some state-of-the-art technology — technology that was to be used years later when the tender arctic terrain was to be assaulted by oil and gas activity.

"We put in the first surface air strip at Inuvik," said Reg. "We were told we couldn't work in the Arctic during the winter months . . . but we worked up there the whole winter long, because we had to.

"We put nine feet of crushed rock on top of the perma-frost, and we sealed the perma-frost right into the ground. That perma-frost hasn't deteriorated a bit, because there's nine feet of crushed rock on top of it for insulation," said Reg with a wide grin.

Chapter Ten

A Legacy of Good Men & Women

REG AND MERV constantly enthused over their ability to surround themselves with good people. It was understood and often articulated that a solid support staff is essential to the development of any business.

Such men and women on the Standard crew included a long list of stalwarts including construction foremen Art Wylie, Frank Logelin and Ernie McGrandle, who were anchor men who could ramrod a job and meet deadlines as if by magic. A successful construction man needs a will of iron, the constitution of an ox and the ability to get the best out of the workers through motivation and leadership.

And there were women who made a mighty contribution to the building of Standard Gravel. Clara McCorkle was a cook who hired on with Standard at Beddington Camp just adjacent to what is now Calgary International Airport. It was during the time Reg and Merv obtained their first contracts on grading and leveling the airport then known as McCall field. Around Clara's kitchen there was no nonsense. Her job was to feed the construction men and the trucking crews, and in her interpretation of that responsibility there was no idle conversation or loitering in the cook's shack. Eat and get back to work or suffer her wrath. Clara remained with Standard for almost thirty years, until her retirement. She died at Fort MacLeod in 1980.

And then there was Lena Audrey Millicent Smith, better known as Smitty. Everybody called her Smitty, and she was around from day one. In the early days, Smitty ran the office with an iron fist, and she was very reluctant to dole out what meager sums of money were lying around.

One day in the early history of the company, Reg's wife Beth arrived at the office looking for a small advance on Reg's weekly paycheck so she could pick up some groceries. No dice, and Smitty was adamant, there was no spare money and Beth would just have to wait until pay day.

"But I don't even have street car fare to get home," pleaded Beth.

So Smitty gave her a street car ticket.

One of the figures to graduate from the Standard Gravel roster was Bill Pratt, son of Ford Pratt, the Ottawa senior civil servant who assisted Reg and Merv in their early marketing missions to the nation's capitol. Bill came west as a youngster and was given a job as a timekeeper on one of the gravel crushing crews. Bill joined the firm in 1948, and went directly to one of the camps an event he recalled vividly.

"I had been in army camps, so I had a basis for comparison. The cabin I lived in was about the size of an average living room. It was constructed of wood frame, with a black tar paper exterior. There was sufficient light, and it contained six bunks with a big old coal and wood stove in the middle of it.

"The wash house was off to the side. It was a dip your own water out of the bucket, run it in the sink, wash your face and hands and throw the bucket outside. For a shower, the procedure called for mixing the hot water with some cold in an overhead bucket, pull the plug and stand under it until empty. Primitive but effective," Pratt recalled.

To wash clothes, the men simply scrubbed them in the river or a nearby pond.

Pratt fondly remembered Ma McCorkle's offerings at the cook tent.

"I'd eat three T-bone steaks for dinner and two helpings of potatoes, and two helpings of vegetables . . . it was a camp joke about how much I used to eat . . . often Ma would make a pumpkin pie with my name inscribed in whipped cream."

Bill said it was not uncommon to see a workman eat seven pork chops at a sitting.

"Good food, awful good food."

Even in the early days, the men always had sheets and blankets, and they were allowed to turn their sheets in once a week for clean ones.

It was the widely recognized opinion of construction people that a large part of the secret of running a successful construction operation is to have a good cook and good food.

"Art Wiley taught me that lesson," Pratt said. "When I came off the Windermere Highway job, they sent me down to Irvine (on the TransCanada Highway east of Medicine Hat) as a foreman.

"I favored the idea of looking after myself first, but Art Wylie disabused me of that idea, and I'll never forget his advice. It was Art's dictum that when you get to be the boss, the men come first, and the boss looks after his own needs last. When the men are settled in tents, working hard all day, they're entitled to a good kitchen, good food and the best of everything.

If there was ever a doubt between the foreman and the worker, always give the worker the benefit of the doubt."

Doug Hetchler, Silver Springs plant, 1970

In Bill Pratt's opinion, the success of Standard Gravel is somehow rooted in the contrasting personalities of Reg and Merv.

It was Pratt's observation that Reg was extremely conscientious about supervising the operation, the administration and the finances.

"This was the unselfish part of Reg Jennings, he purposely kept a low profile to allow Red an even higher profile."

It was a magnificent team effort. Red watched for the big jobs. Reg did the economics, figured the bids, the financing, the equipment requirements, the manpower and all the details. Merv took all of the assembled material to Ottawa and obtained the contracts.

Pratt recalls an early experience with Dutton in 1948, when the Calgary Stampeders invaded Toronto as the Western Canada representative in the Grey Cup.

"I had worked for Standard in 1948, and returned to Ottawa that winter to go back to school. Red called my dad and asked him to bring me along to Toronto for the Grey Cup game. He had extra tickets. My dad and I arrived in Toronto and met Mr. Dutton in his room at the Royal York Hotel. We were leaving for the game, and Mr. Dutton said: 'You're going to be cold Bill.'"

Pratt was curious about Dutton's sudden concern about his comfort when a huge black coat was thrust over his shoulder.

"You're going to be cold, Bill . . . wear the coat," said Mr. Dutton.

"Gee I don't think so, Mr. Dutton," said Pratt.

"I put the coat on and I damned near buckled at the knees. He had all the pockets loaded with bottles. This was the portable bar, and I was the carrier. So I got the best seat in the house, because I was right in the middle of the row on the 55-yard line, passing drinks in both directions.

"Dutton won $27,000 on that game. I collected the bets. $27,000 in those days . . . I could hardly comprehend that kind of money."

"Innovative, inspiring, personal, gentle . . . those are the kind of words I would use to describe Reg," said Pratt.

"I was impatient, even though I was doing well, I always wanted to do something new, something different, something exciting, and that's probably why I had seventeen jobs in twenty-one years with that company.

"When I'd get a little frustrated within the organization, I'd go up and rap timidly on Reg's door. There he was sitting behind the desk, not a big man in stature but he looked awful big to me as I approached him with my concern. He made me welcome, allowed me to talk freely, and we would chat openly about my family."

Then Reg would gesture toward the bottom left hand drawer of his desk.

"I've got it here, Bill. All the plans are in here. You've got nothing to worry about. Bill . . . we're going to move you up the line. Don't worry about the wages, they'll come."

"Reg had a way of renewing an employee's confidence in himself . . . make you feel important . . . picked you right up."

L-R: Reg Jennings, Angus McLellean and a Chrysler salesman

On another occasion Pratt was asked to drive Reg to the Calgary airport for one of his frequent business trips to the East.

"It was in the early 1950s, and I drove him from the office to the airport in a nice new Pontiac. I'll never forget that conversation."

"You're doing a good job Bill," said Reg. "Keep it up . . . you're really important to us."

"He made me feel like the only guy that ever worked for the company," Pratt remembered. "And then as he stepped out of the car at the airport, he said to me: 'By the way, you better keep this car because you're going to need one.'"

It was the first car Pratt ever owned, and he was overwhelmed by the gesture. Later, when Pratt had gotten used to the idea of driving a company car, he was transferred out of Calgary to a remote construction site, and turned the car in at the office. Reg spoke firmly.

"You can't leave your wife at home without a car," he said.

And that was typical of Reg.

"He made you feel like you were really important to the thing. It was the way he developed loyalty. Loyalty was built into all of us." It is Pratt's opinion that Reg was a masterful handler of people, and it was often a very personal relationship he developed with the employees.

One day Pratt was at his desk, just outside Reg's door. At the time, his job was supervisor of timekeepers for the entire operation and some of his responsibility was to cost out projects.

Jennings would designate on a pad of paper the various units of cost: a cost for dirt per yard; culvert per foot and all of the various elements.

It was Pratt's job to do the extensions, e.g. 200,000 yards of dirt at nineteen cents per yard equals $38,000.

"When I finally got all the numbers together, and a final number at the bottom of the page, I would proudly march into Reg's office with the completed calculation."

Reg would then make a few adjustments and ask for a re-calculation, and back Pratt would go for another calculation.

"I would turn the figures in again, confident Reg would find them acceptable."

"You're getting close Bill," he would say.

"And back we would go again. Reg worked those figures down so fine, I swear he knew every pebble of gravel that went into those jobs."

On another occasion, Reg asked Pratt into his office for a personal discussion on his family life.

Doug Shaut, 1972

"How's Millie?" Reg would ask. "How's the baby?"

"What are you doing about a house?"

"You've got a growing family Bill, you'd better get yourself a house."

"I don't have the money just yet," replied Bill. At the time Pratt was earning about $250 per month.

"Don't worry about the money," said Jennings. "You go and find a house, then come and see me."

Pratt proceeded to search out a neat, three-bedroom bungalow in a nice district, close to a riding stable where his wife could enjoy her passion for horseback riding.

"Good buy, nice area," said Reg. "How much do you need?"

Pratt needed $3,500 to complete the deal and Reg wrote him a cheque. He was dumbfounded.

"You just don't give away $3,500," I said. "I'll make arrangements to pay you back."

Every once in awhile Pratt would bring up the $3,500 and offer to pay it back, but Reg would deftly change the subject. If Reg didn't want to deal with a certain subject, he could stonewall it indefinitely.

Several years later Pratt went to him and said: "Reg, we've got to clean it up."

"No Bill," came the reply. "You've paid that debt off lots of times."

During his twenty-one years of employment with Standard Gravel, exposed to every facet of the operation, Bill Pratt gained a thorough understanding of each partner's strengths, weaknesses, fortes and idiosyncracies.

Chinook Shopping Centre · *Glenbow Archives*

Dutton was a man of immense will and a powerful personality.

"You would wonder how the hell he could get away with some of the things he did. Just the strength of his personality I guess," pondered Pratt.

Dutton was impulsive. Pratt recalled the time he was flying in one of the company's aircraft. Red was dressed for warmth with a heavy overcoat.

The cabin began to heat up, and there was no way to reduce the engine heat in the cabin while the plane was flying. Dutton was sweltering, the sweat pouring down his neck, and you could see he was about to explode.

"When we get on the ground, I'm going to get rid of this goddamn flying Turkish bath."

When the plane landed, Merv headed straight for the airplane sales office.

"I want a new airplane," he said to the man.

"All we have on hand is the blue and white Piper Apache out there," said the salesman.

"I'll take it," said Dutton.

And that was the end of that. No discussion with Reg, no sleeping on it overnight. With Dutton, the deal has to be made right now. He had no patience.

Bill Pratt is convinced that in spite of Dutton's powerful personality, Jennings always had the final say on the job site.

Pratt was the project manager of the massive Chinook Shopping Centre project in Calgary. After the job was completed and the stores were open, it was decided to extend the complex and close in the mall. A big glass wall was going in and just to protect it during construction a large plywood shell was built around it.

On Reg's orders, Pratt instructed the superintendent to paint it, and make it match the rest of the décor.

"I told him three days in a row, and three days in a row, my orders were countermanded," said Pratt.

Pratt confronted the superintendent after the third day and asked him who was countermanding the order to paint the plywood.

"Here he comes now," said the superintendent, pointing to Dutton, who was touring the mall with a couple of bank officials.

When Dutton arrived, Pratt buttonholed him.

"Mr. Dutton, I've got a problem," said Pratt.

"Yeah, what's your problem?" he asked.

"That plywood over there, three days in a row I told the superintendent to paint it, and three days in a row you told him not to paint it."

"That's right," said Dutton.

"Then you bastards better make up your minds who the hell is running this goddamn job," said Pratt.

"You are," he said and turned to walk away with his banker friends. In a moment later he turned in Pratt's direction, and in a loud voice said: "Did you hear what that little son of a bitch said to me?"

But the point was made. Dutton knew damned well that Reg wanted the plywood painted, and he wasn't going to argue the point any further.

Dutton's antics on the job sites were memorable.

On the Windermere Highway job which intersected with the TransCanada eighteen miles east of Lake Louise and followed the Kootenay Valley to Radium, Dutton made several appearances. It was cost-plus job, and Merv seemed to get a kick out of visiting the job.

Because of the difficulty of the terrain, the latest model caterpillar had been purchased for the job. It had a semi-automatic clutch which was very effective but tricky to operate.

Dutton showed up and was watching the cat skinner as he gingerly maneuvered his machine, removing a chunk of dirt at a time until he finally chewed out the beginnings of a trench to form a culvert.

It wasn't good enough for Dutton. It was too slow. He fired the cat skinner on the spot, and climbed up on the machine. He knew nothing of the new clutch arrangement.

Pratt was pounding stakes across the roadway and he could hear the gears grinding, and Dutton cursing. He couldn't make the cat go forwards or backwards.

In the meantime, the cat skinner had picked up his belongings, and he was walking down the road, about 100 yards from the scene.

By this time Dutton was standing up on the seat yelling at the top of his voice.

"Get back here you son-of-a-bitch, you're hired."

"I swear to God," said Pratt, "that Dutton just got a kick out of stirring things up."

One day Dutton visited a road construction on which Charlie McLean was the foreman.

He complained about the foreslope, the ditch slope, the crown wasn't right. Nothing about the job was right, and Dutton was fuming and rasping.

"How is she for length?" asked Charlie. "Dutton broke up laughing."

Early in his career, Pratt was doing the survey work for Standard as part of his training program. He and another rookie were lying down on the edge of the road, sighting down a set of sticks.

"You can measure all you want, but the final test is to get down on your belly and eyeball them . . . I'm lying down in the grade instructing the other guy to move the stake this way or that, and suddenly right beside me a car slams on the brakes and showers me with gravel.

"It was Dutton. He jumped out of the car. 'I caught you. I caught you lying down on the job.'

"I tried to explain it to him, but he didn't want to listen to an explanation.

"Then he argues that the stakes are wrong, the grade is wrong, everything he sees is wrong.

"I pull out my field book and show him all the measurements are correct, and in frustration, I finally said, 'why the hell don't you take off and leave me alone?'

"At that, he starts to laugh like hell, and he jumps in the car and drives away.

"That's typical Dutton."

For the outsider, the great mystery was how Reg and Merv could get along together – Dutton volatile and impetuous – Reg, quiet, efficient, methodical, thoughtful.

"It was a mystery to all of us," said Pratt. "I was there twenty-one years, and all the time I was there we took our instructions from Jennings."

Reg made the calculations and ran the jobs. He arranged the financing, bought the equipment, and supervised the manpower.

Dutton was the front man. If officials from Ottawa or somewhere else wanted to see the job, Merv took them in tow, toured them around the job sites and entertained them. He was a master showman.

It was a classic case of two direct opposites fitting together perfectly, and never a harsh word between them.

Building up the business wasn't without its problems. Reg and Merv were not immune to a periodic error in judgment. Fortunately, they made many more good business decisions than they did bad ones. One bad one was their venture into an automobile dealership.

During that period of rapid expansion and growth of the companies in the 1950s and 1960s, Reg and Merv found themselves, inadvertently, the owner of a promising, but struggling General Motors dealership.

Don MacKay, the ex-Mayor of Calgary, had an opportunity to pick up a General Motors Sales franchise, but he needed backers.

Dutton thought it would be a good opportunity for his son Norman.

"We set up a company called Stampede Motors," Reg recalled, "but I can't remember how the equity was proportioned. Anyway, Merv had some, I had some and Norman and Don MacKay had some as the operators of the business. All we were, in a sense, were silent backers."

It turned out that MacKay and Norman were not getting along well, and expense accounts and the costs of doing business were considered to be far out of proportion to the amount of sales revenue being generated.

"I pulled the plug on them," Merv said. "This goddamn thing is going to stop right now . . . there must be a conflict of personalities here."

Suddenly, Reg and Merv were in the car business, so they hired a manager who convinced them the secret was in volume sales and low mark-ups.

"All he could think about was making $100 a car," Reg remembered. "You can't make any money selling cars at $100 mark-up, I can tell you that.

"Then the General Manager of G.M. in Oshawa arrived in Calgary, and he has just the right guy for us to put into Stampede Motors – Hartley from Winnipeg," Reg said.

"Good old Hartley," said Merv. "Everything went up and nothing came down. Then we had the job of getting rid of Hartley.

"After we got rid of Hartley, we got a fellow named John Cummings, who was also recommended by General Motors.

"Poor old John Cummings, who had recovered from a drinking problem, did a helluva job, really brought the thing out of the weeds – had the thing in a good profitable position, and goddamnit if he didn't go out one night and get drunk and kill himself."

Enthusiasm for the automobile business was on the wane. The boys eventually sold the business and kept the building and property.

In another venture into uncharted waters, Jennings and Dutton got into the oil business and into pipeline contracting. Bill Knode, a pioneer oilman in Turner Valley, formed a company called Grizzly Petroleums.

"It wasn't too successful," Reg remembered, "but we didn't get in too deep.

"When pipeline work first started in Canada, we organized Canadian Pipe Line Construction, with the thought in mind of having a Canadian corporation that could do pipeline work.

"At that time, U.S. firms were coming in and grabbing all the Canadian pipeline contracts," Reg said.

The company never really got off the ground because of the difficulty in finding qualified pipeline personnel, particularly welders. Eventually a partnership arrangement was reached with Williams Brothers, one of the world's largest pipeline contractors, based in Tulsa, Oklahoma.

"We did a helluva lot of work with them, but all we did was invest our money in it," Reg said.

The Dutton-Williams firm built parts of the West Coast Transmission line in British Columbia. "We built a couple of pump stations for them through Burns and Dutton," Reg said. "They turned out alright, the ones we did on our own – but the ones we did in partnership with Williams Brothers were disasterous."

Burns and Dutton supplied all the concrete for about 1,000 miles of pipeline, and all the river crossings. Large weights, made of concrete, are affixed to the pipeline on river crossings and act as anchors holding the pipe on the bottom of the river.

The pipeline company did some business around Edmonton, and participated, to a large extent, in the construction of the Texaco Refinery in that city.

One of the most unhappy experiences was the 1,500 miles of pipeline construction for Inland Natural Gas in British Columbia. It was a small-diameter line, designed to carry natural gas from a plant in the B.C. interior to consumers in the Prince Rupert region.

"It was a sad experience," Reg said.

"Sad experience. It was $2 million worth of sadness, wasn't it?" interjected Merv.

"We got into some tough country, under power lines which hadn't been investigated by Williams Brothers thoroughly enough to see what we were up against. We were in rock, and every foot of that pipeline had to be padded," Merv recalled.

Reg described the operation style of Guy Connors, the man assigned to run the job for Williams Brothers.

"He was a great high-roller, but he never thought about what it would cost. He'd go off to get a back-hoe and instead of getting one, he'd get three. And if he was short of men, Christ, he'd send to Saudi Arabia and fly them over here.

"I was only on the site two or three times," Reg remembered. "I was too busy trying to raise money to keep the job running."

Merv recalled that Connors had established a reputation as one of the country's greatest pipe-liners. In fact, he started his construction career with Merv's father on railway construction.

"He could get a job done, and he had ten men doing two men's work," Merv said.

"When we formed the partnership," Reg said, "we called the company Dutton, Williams Bros. Limited.

"The first goddamn thing they did was rent a fancy suite of offices in downtown Calgary with palm trees and thick carpets."

"Yeah, we lost more than $2 million on the job," Merv recalled with a look of chagrin. "That Connors. He'd get up at three o'clock in the morning, and get on long distance, and would call every job they had going in the world – no matter where it was – Saudi Arabia – South Africa – Venezuela . . . and we were paying the telephone bills.

"That was the way they operated, but they found out they couldn't operate in Canada like that."

Merv and Reg were convinced they should have been able to develop one of Canada's major pipeline construction companies, but the experience in B.C. soured them at least temporarily . . . and besides, the rest of the operation was expanding in all directions.

"I've said it before, and I'll say it again," said Merv, "if we'd had the proper instruction and the proper men, we'd have done all right on pipelines. But you can't be second in anything – second prize is for losers."

There were other ventures. Some were so far removed from the construction and gravel business, Reg and Merv have difficulty remembering anything about them. One obscure investment was in the box manufacturing business. They had taken advantage of this magnificent opportunity to make wooden pallets, butter boxes, egg crates and assorted wooden boxes. Unfortunately it was at a time when wooden boxes were being replaced by the cheaper, more efficient and more popular cardboard cartons.

"Wooden boxes just passed right out of existence," said Reg with a grin.

And then there was the coal mining venture. It was a strip mining project near Grassy Lake and Taber in the Lethbridge district.

Reg and Merv hired a mine manager and purchased huge rubber-tired earth movers to strip the over-burden away from the coal seams. At the peak of production, right after the war, they had two tipples running and were shipping several rail cars daily to keep up with their contract.

"I forgot all about that goddamn thing," said Dutton.

"We operated the mine for about three years and then sold out to Mannix," Reg remembers.

John Denholm, who remembered the anguish of some of the losses, recalled a contract to build a dam for Seattle Light and Power in Washington State. It was a joint venture with Morrison-Knudsen, an American construction giant and Mannix of Calgary. Standard's role in the $33 million job was to install the giant metal flues to transport water to the turbines. The flue pipes were fabricated in Denmark, and arrived about twenty feet short of specifications. That and some other problems resulted in a loss in excess of ten million dollars, which was shared proportionately by the partners.

LEGEND CLAIMS that a farmer in the mid-western United States created the first drive-in theatre in the early 1940s by hanging a screen between two telephone poles. He used a foghorn for a speaker and charged a quarter a car.

Whatever its history, the drive-in theatre, fondly remembered as the "passion pit", came to Western Canada in the late forties and it was the pioneering spirit of Reg and Merv that provided the enormously popular combination of privacy and entertainment centered around the automobile.

An enthusiastic, and innovative pioneer of Canada's motion picture business sold them on the idea during the Grey Cup revelries of 1948. Frank Kershaw of Winnipeg was intrigued with the meteoric rise in automobile registrations in Western Canada, and perspicaciously noted that drive-in movie theatres which had begun to appear in the U.S. mid-west and in California had not yet been adopted in Western Canada.

As the wild-west delegation from Calgary, with their horses, chuck-wagons, western bands and invincible Stampeder football team stormed the benign burgers of Toronto, Kershaw did his best to explain the drive-in theatre opportunity to Reg and Merv. Above the noise of the crowd they received his message, but they convinced him to re-direct his enthusiam to the festivities at hand and they would pursue the opportunity after the Stampeders had secured the Grey Cup for the deserving citizens of Calgary and surrounding environs.

Shortly after their return from the Grey Cup in 1948, Reg, Merv and Frank Kershaw headed for California to study the emerging phenomenon of drive-in theatres.

"We headed out in an airplane for California," Merv remembered. "We met every son-of-a-bitch in the drive-in theatre business in California, and boy they were going like hot-cakes down there."

Reg and Merv were convinced they had indeed found a bejeweled opportunity, one which would absorb their passion for entrepreneurial innovation. They were equally convinced that Kershaw was the man to pilot the project through its birth and development.

Frank had grown up in the business. His fascinating career spanned silent serials, the advent of talkies, and Canada's first big world movie premiere.

The soft-spoken Westerner (he was born in England, but moved to Winnipeg with his parents in 1905) talked endlessly about the spectacular growth of the movie industry.

Frank was a youngster of nine when his father opened one of the first silent movie houses in Winnipeg in 1913. "I was the envy of all my classmates," he once said.

Typically the opportunity to see the latest in two-reel Westerns carried responsibilities. He served as an usher. "With no dialogue to clutter up the plot, the stress was on action. Sound effects were created by the piano player. Later, Dad added a drummer who could switch at will from gunfire to thundering hooves."

In 1945, following a stint in the Vancouver office of Famous Players, Mr. Kershaw was transferred to Toronto as General Manager of General Theatre Supply Company and Theatre Confections Ltd. His job: the setting up of the first confection company operated by Famous Players. Candy and popcorn counters popped up in FP theatres across the country.

Mr. Kershaw resigned from Famous Players in 1946 in order to become a manufacturers' agent with franchises for the Canadian distribution of vending machines. He also had a candy distribution company.

In semi-retirement on a three-acre Vancouver estate, he decided to strike out for Calgary when an embargo on U.S. imports crippled his business.

He made the connection with Merv and Reg, and following the Grey Cup week-end soon found himself the third man on a whirlwind tour of Southern California.

"So we came back to Calgary, because now we knew what we wanted," said Merv. "Kershaw knew all about projectors and he knew what he had to do."

"Reg," said Merv, with a teasing wink, "now we're ready to go – where do we get the money?"

"I don't know," came the reply, "but let's go down to Toronto and see what we can do."

Off they went to Toronto with Kershaw and Ross Henderson, the accountant. Harold Millican, the lawyer, also a partner, stayed home. The Calgary group appeared before the Board of The Toronto-Dominion Bank, a stern-faced, pin-striped battalion of Bay Street tycoons who were totally bewildered by all the enthusiasm for an outdoor movie house – something called a "drive-in."

"We were asking for $350,000, and they wanted to know what in hell this drive-in business was all about," Merv recalled.

Fortunately, Bob Ray, the president of the bank, had been to a drive-in movie near Toronto, and was sold on the idea.

One of the bank directors whispered to Dutton during the meeting: "Tell me Red, are they really passion pits?"

"I don't know, I haven't been to one. I'll tell you better after we build one," Merv replied.

The bank forwarded the money with a noticeable absence of enthusiasm, and the Calgary foursome headed westward, convinced they were on the verge of a bonanza.

The next task was to secure a location. There was a twenty-acre plot on the northwest corner of MacLeod Trail and 66th Avenue. In 1948, it was on the southern outskirts of Calgary.

Reg proceeded with the negotiations, and eventually purchased the plot for $1,200 an acre. In 1948, he considered this an exhorbitant sum, but the location was correct for the project.

It turned out that they were also able to acquire twelve acres closer to the city, but it was separated by an eight-acre plot that was littered with car bodies and assorted junk.

The partners, Kershaw and Henderson, balked on the purchase of the additional parcels. They were worried about getting in "too deep" on an untried and unproved venture. At least it was untried and unproved in Western Canada.

"Let's buy the goddamn thing," Merv insisted. "I don't want a junkyard next to the theatre . . . it's bad for business."

So they bought it.

The additional parcel of land provided plenty of room for access, parking and expansion.

Construction of the Calgary theatre, to be known as the Chinook Drive-In, began immediately following the land acquisition.

There were no bids tendered on the construction phase of the development. Arnold Berg, a project foreman for Standard Gravel, was assigned the task of designing and engineering the theatre. Standard Gravel was given the site preparation, surfacing and paving, while the construction of the giant screen and facilities buildings was awarded to Burns and Dutton Construction.

Berg's screen measured fifty-seven by forty-five feet, and was affixed to twin seventy-foot towers. The entire assembly was anchored to the ground with 216 tons of concrete, and was designed to withstand winds in excess of 100 miles per hour.

Other than the ticket office at the entrance gate, the only other structure on the twenty-acre site was the screen and the projection building, which also housed the washrooms and snack bar. The paved ramps, shaped in a series of semi-circles in front of the screen, provided accommodation for about 1,000 cars. Beside each car was a post, with loudspeaker attached. The speakers connected to the central sound system, were clipped inside the car window, and each patron controlled his own volume.

The first movie that played at the Chinook Drive-In was *The Perils of Pauline*, a classic vintage melodrama.

It was a beautiful June evening. The lights of Calgary to the north began to twinkle against the darkening summer sky. To the south, the natural gas flares of Turner Valley danced in ghostly splendor.

Reg, Merv, Kershaw, Berg and Henderson were waiting for the curtain to rise on the Chinook's premier performance. The ads were on the radio and in the newspapers,

Chinook Drive-In Theatre ·
Glenbow Archives

everything was in readiness. Merv was pacing impatiently near the projection booth, worried whether Calgarians would accept the outdoor theatre. He glanced northward. A column of cars, bumper-to-bumper, snaked across the cemetery hill and along the Macleod Trail.

One by one they turned into the drive-in. Mostly loaded with mom, dad, the kids and often the family dog, they swarmed the opening performance.

"It was the damnest thing I ever saw," recalled Merv.

Reg still clutches his ribs in laughter when he thinks about it.

"I handed Dutton a flashlight and told him he better get out there and direct traffic, or we'd have the worst snarl-up in Calgary's history."

Dutton proved to be an effective, but ill-tempered and very expressive car park. But the boys were exhilarated. They knew they had struck a responsive chord with the theatre-going public.

The Calgary triumph spurred the group on to a rapid expansion program. Theatres were quickly built in Edmonton and Lethbridge. Less than a year later, Dutton, Jennings and partners were operating the Chinook and Stampede theatres in Calgary; the Starlite and Southside in Edmonton, and the Green Acres in Lethbridge.

The Edmonton Journal, in its typically cumbersome English, was enthusiastic in its welcome of the new entertainment mode to the city:

"For a large percentage of car owners and passengers, drive-ins provide entertainment and social facilities unequalled in the past. The friendly atmosphere of a group together in the car now is further enhanced by the ability to enjoy a 'movie' at the Starlite Drive-In Theatre as part of an evening's outing.

"Normal conversation may be carried on in the car during the show, without having to whisper in order to avoid bothering other patrons. Downtown parking worries also are eliminated."

In Lethbridge, Dutton was called upon to make a speech at the opening ceremonies of the Green Acres in the city.

"The outdoor drive-in theatre has proved tremendously popular all over the United States and Canada," he said. "By next year (1950), there will not be a city in Canada with a population of 20000 and over that will not have a drive-in theatre."

While it was popular with the patrons, the downtown indoor theatre owners were less gracious in their acceptance of the drive-ins. In Lethbridge, the competitors were downright rude, and mustered sufficient clout to prevent the Dutton-Jennings groups from acquiring a regular supply of first-run movies.

Heritage Park · *Glenbow Archives*

The Green Acres in Lethbridge ran some dreadful "B" movies, but the patrons were not to be deterred. The drive-in proved to be a place where the social dimension was equally as important as the entertainment value. At least in its early history, the term "passion pit" was deemed an appropriate appellation.

The locust-spread of television, around 1952, pitched hundreds of conventional indoor movie houses into bankruptcy, but with buck-a-car admissions, the drive-ins survived and flourished. Dusk-to-dawn horror marathons always drew crowds. Any Elvis Presley or James Dean picture filled the ramps.

Each theatre was incorporated as a separate entity and each concession stand became an independent business venture. The drive-ins added significantly to the cash flow of the spreading conglomerate.

In the mid-fifties, Reg built a spacious ranch-style house at the highest point on Eagle Ridge, a district which was being developed as Calgary's most exclusive.

Reg's home overlooked the Glenmore Reservoir, and the Rocky Mountains to the west. The northeast provided an unimpaired view of downtown Calgary. But his favorite view was down the slope to the southwest and the main thoroughfare of Heritage Park and a pioneer village recreated from authentic rural business establishments relocated to the site. Reg was a primary promoter of the park and remained active in its development well into retirement.

Twice daily Reg drove the Glenmore Trail, back and forth from the office in Manchester. The route took him past the Chinook Drive-In.

"Everytime I'd go by, I'd say Jesus what a goddamn waste of land — we have twenty acres — and everytime I'd go by on the way home, I'd say what in the hell are we going to do with the rest of that damned land? It was starting to get more valuable.

"One day, Dutton and I got word that 'Chunky' Woodward had been in town, and was dickering on a piece of property between Elbow Drive and the Macleod Trail on 72nd Avenue."

Woodward was then chief executive of Woodward's Department stores, which had originated in Vancouver.

"We went right to work on 'Chunky' Woodward," Dutton said.

Woodward had purchased the plot at 72nd Avenue and was planning a major shopping centre, with a Woodward's Department Store as the prime feature.

Dutton and Jennings talked him into selling the 72nd Avenue property and relocating at the Chinook location as prime tenant in their shopping centre proposal.

With Woodward as prime tenant, the decision was made. It was early in the 1960s when the huge movie screen, projection building and ramps were demolished to make way for the shopping centre. Again it was the automobile that had created the opportunity. Just as it had revolutionized the theatre business, it was to inflict dramatic changes on shopping patterns. Patrons wanted a place to park and one-stop shopping.

It was modeled after the Oakridge Shopping Centre in Vancouver, at the north end of the Lions' Gate Bridge. It was to be one of the largest in Canada, with more than seventy-five retail stores and related businesses and an eight-storey medical building, at a cost more than $20 million.

It was Frank Kershaw who was assigned the managing director of Chinook, responsible for co-ordination of design, leasing and construction of the $8,000,000 project, with plenty of help from Reg and Merv.

When forty-two Calgary doctors and twelve dentists moved into the Chinook Professional Building in the spring of 1966, they were testing the theory that patients prefer to attend to their medical and dental needs – as well as do their household shopping – in a suburban shopping centre. It was the only medical centre of its size in Canada located in a regional shopping centre.

Layout of the shopping centre and medical building was the result of an enormous amount of research. From extensive studies on similar projects across the U.S.A. and Canada, Chinook quickly gained the reputation as the most up-to-the-minute shopping complex and medical office facility in North America.

In short order, detailed plans and specifications were produced for a centre that would accommodate the latest improvements in professional buildings, making every allowance for special plumbing, specially-provided duct-work and electrical outlets for medical and dental equipment. Also drawn into their plans were facilities for a modern communications system between offices, darkrooms for dental offices, high-intensity glare-free lighting, tinted windows and an even higher degree of controlled air conditioning than that required in normal offices.

Bill Pratt, a hard-driving and ambitious young employee with the Standard Gravel Group, was named construction superintendent of the project.

Dutton was fascinated with the prospect of being a principal in one of the country's largest shopping mall complexes. Every day, he was on the site at 8 a.m., watching every move and supervising the progress brick-by-brick and board-by-board.

Frequently he toured visitors through the maze of the construction site.

"One day I brought a group of bankers down to tour the site, and I spotted a young workman leaning on a shovel.

"We walked the length of the complex, in and out of partially built stores, and I kept one eye on this young fellow. For a half-hour he leaned on that shovel and didn't make a move.

"Finally I couldn't stand it any longer, and I walked over and spoke to him.

"Who is your supervisor, young man?"

"I don't have a supervisor," came the reply. "Who are you?" he enquired of Red.

"Well I'm the guy that's running this job, and you can go and turn your time and pick up your pay because you're fired," I said.

"You can't fire me," he answered.

"Why can't I?" I asked.

"Because I work for the telephone company, that's why," he said with a grin.

Red walked away fuming, but there was nothing he could do about it. For years, Red told the story on himself and roared with laughter each time he repeated it.

Frank Kershaw eventually retired to California, and in keeping with his zest for activity operated an avocado farm as a hobby. He died tragically in a mid-air crash near the Canary Islands while vacationing in 1976.

Chapter Thirteen

Time Off

WORK AND PLAY WERE ALL THE SAME to Merv and Reg. Social life and business life were one. The basic element was energy — whether it was all-out effort on a project or a determined public relations campaign in search of new business — and there seemed to be no limit to their output.

They had a deep appreciation of each other's humor, and were constantly playing practical jokes on one another. Often they would team up for a gag on somebody else.

The first recorded incident of Reg's modest revelry occurred on Christmas Eve in 1934. He was on his way home, after a brief session of seasonal good-will with some of his workmates. Driving a relatively new Ford of the era, he hit a patch of ice and skidded into a Calgary street car in the Hillhurst district. The case was covered in the Calgary Herald.

"A jug full of Christmas cheer figured in the case of Reginald Jennings, who was charged with negligent driving, following the collision of his auto and a street car. But it turned out the bottled cheer had nothing to do with the accident.

"Jennings was fined $15 without costs and the jug was returned to him.

"Constable Joseph Strange said that he found the jug, corked and practically full, lying on its side in the bottom of the auto. Jennings had not been drinking and was perfectly sober. The officer stated that the crash might have been responsible for the breaking of the seal on the jug. After the fine had been levied, M.H. Staples, court prosecutor, asked: 'What about the jug?'

"'Oh that's all right, I'll take it as my fee,' interposed G.W.H. Millican, who appeared for Jennings.

"Amid a ripple of laughter, Magistrate Scott ordered the jug returned to Mr. Jennings, and Mr. Staples solemnly handed the bottled goods over to the owner."

Shortly after they teamed up to form the construction firm, Reg and Merv sponsored a senior baseball team in Calgary. The ball team evolved partly from Dutton's compulsion to be involved with sports, and partly because he convinced Reg that there may be a few dollars profit if all went well.

Members of the ball team included such legendary sport figures as Lorne Carr, Dodger Lewis, Joe McGoldrick, Tiny and Paul Thompson and Dutton himself.

An African-American touring team from the United States appeared one Sunday to challenge Dutton's group, and it was agreed the two teams would split the receipts from a silver collection. Dutton was in charge of the financial arrangements, a situation which still causes Reg to shudder when he dares to reflect on it.

The game was played at Calgary's downtown Mewata Stadium in front of a good turnout of Calgary fans.

Dutton's job, after the game, was to count the money, pay the expenses and split the remainder between the two teams. As he was paying off the captain of the visiting team, he deducted for stadium rent; he deducted for posters and publicity; he deducted for umpire's fees; and he deducted for some lost baseballs.

The burly black captain fondled the paltry, few remaining dollars and muttered: "Man, I've never seen so many 'deducts' anywhere."

"We didn't make any money in baseball," said Reg. "All we did was pay money."

"Then we got into the horse-racing business."

The partners possessed a deep fondness for racehorses, but in their early naivete, neither could be accused of having much horse sense in the evaluation of horseflesh.

It was spring of 1950, and the construction business was thriving.

"A friend of ours was explaining to me the endless opportunities in the horse raising game," Reg remembered.

"The strategy was to watch for the claiming races and pick up a fine string of racehorses by claiming them at bargain-basement prices.

"Before we knew it, Dutton and I had a stable of six horses, each representing about a $2,000 investment.

"We fed them quality hay and oats, we nursed them, we paid to have them exercised, we paid for their shelter, and we paid all their medical bills.

"But they didn't win any races," said Reg.

One day, after what seemed to be a lifetime of paying out without any return, Merv and Red decided to liquidate their race horse assets. They engaged Don Ball, the well-known Edmonton auctioneer to dispose of the entire stable.

For years Reg kept the receipt from the auctioneer. It is a reminder to him that fools often tread on territory that angels avoid like the plague.

```
THE AUCTIONEERS SALE LISTS
SIX HORSES AND THE PRICES
RECEIVED AT AUCTION:


HEART ATTACK           $150
NORTH LOVE             $225
LOVE WELL              $320
RED BLAZE              $345
LILLOET BOY        $NO SALE
REASON ISOLADA     $NO SALE
TOTAL PROCEEDS       $1,040
5% COMMISSION         $-52
EXPENSES              $-24
CHEQUE HEREWITH
FOR NET PROCEEDS:      $964
```

"It was an expensive pastime," said Reg.

In another venture into play land, Reg and Merv ended up with a 113-foot yacht, which they kept moored at Vancouver Harbor.

"It was like this," said Merv. "Reg and Jay (McLaughlin) were down in California cavorting around the countryside and I was back in Calgary looking after some other business.

"I had to go over to Vancouver for something, so I climbed on the airplane at the Calgary airport and Max Bell was sitting there.

"'Merv,' said Max, 'I've got a boat out at the coast, and I think you fellows should buy it. Hell, you fellows could have a great time with it.' So I agreed to have a look at it. I didn't know the first thing about boats, but it looked pretty good to me, so I agreed to take it.

"The next thing I did was contact Jennings and McLaughlin. I found them in Palm Springs.

"'When are you fellows coming home?' I asked."

"Monday," was the reply.

"You'd better come Sunday," said Merv. "I've got a big deal on for you."

"What is it?" they asked.

"I can't tell you over the telephone," said Merv. "You'll have to get up here and have a look at the proposition," he told them.

Dutton could tell they were all excited. They thought he had lined up yet another large contract. Jay and Reg began their journey to Vancouver, and after changing planes and flying all night, they landed in Vancouver the next morning.

"Where are we going?" asked Reg as he stepped off the plane.

"Just get your bags in the car, and we'll drive you out there," said Merv.

Dutton had instructed the driver to take them directly to the dock and put their bags on board. He had pre-arranged with the captain to be prepared for an immediate departure on a hand signal. Merv, Reg and Jay were on the boat for a few seconds when it began to slip away from the jetty and out into Vancouver harbor.

"These guys were dog-tired from traveling," said Merv. "So I slipped them a couple of snorts to get them relaxed."

"We had a cracker-jack of a cook on board, and I had him prepare an outstanding spread for lunch."

McLaughlin had been looking everything over, and eventually said: "This is really pretty nice."

"Do you really like it, Jay?" Merv asked him.

"I sure do," he replied.

Reg had been out walking around the deck and looking things over when he returned to the group and said: "This is quite a thing . . . we could have a great time on this."

"Well," said Merv, "I sure as hell hope you enjoy it because I just bought it for you."

By this time, Dutton was doubled with laughter.

"That was Dutton's idea of a good joke," said Reg.

The Jormholm

"We worked all night to get to Vancouver, then he fills us up on booze and spreads out a gourmet lunch . . . and springs this on us."

The boat was to be known as the Jormholm. It was named after a company the partners had incorporated in Great Falls, Montana-Jorm Incorporated. J for Jay McLaughlin;

O for Ossie McIntyre; R for Reg Jennings and M for Merv Dutton. It was decided to call it the Jormholm, and some time after that, it was discovered that the word was Norwegian for four men on a raft.

On the first Christmas morning after they had acquired the Jormholm, Merv received a telephone call at his Calgary home, informing him there had been a serious fire on the boat.

"The crew had a party, and some drunk bastard had taken a cigarette and dropped it into a plastic container in the galley," said Merv.

Total damage was about $185,000, which was covered by insurance. The partners put another $5,000 on top of that and turned it into one of the most luxurious yachts on the west coast.

The main cabin, lounge and dining area was completely glassed in for a 360-degree view. The captain's quarters were on the deck above, and the sleeping accommodation was all below. It was driven by two large diesel engines, 254 horsepower each.

Jay McLaughlin, in the summer of 1956, commandeered the Jormholm for a trip to Lake Washington at Seattle. He wanted to entertain a group of his Montana and Washington friends at the Gold Cup speed boat races on Lake Washington. There were fifty-six people on the boat for cocktails and a buffet dinner.

"Some of the happiest days of my life were on that boat," said Dutton. "I loved it, and I loved the British Columbia coast. Today, if I had that boat I would live on it the year round."

The Jormholm was used for business and pleasure, with Reg assigned the responsibility of figuring out an accounting system.

"It was a masterful job of accounting to handle this thing," said Reg. "I had the job for awhile, and I finally got rid of it to a guy in Vancouver.

"We used to get the volume of whatever it costs us, and then we could work out a figure per day. If Dutton was on it for pleasure, we would charge him whatever the daily costs were – about $400 a day. If it was used for a business trip – to entertain clients – we kept a separate log for the income tax department.

On two separate occasions, the partners sailed the Jormholm down the west coast to Mexico. They were anchored at La Paz on the Baja Peninsula when Jay McLaughlin took a notion he wanted to go ashore and make a phone call. He reversed the engines and burned out a crankshaft at a location thousands of miles from the nearest mechanical help.

Importing mechanics into Mexico, even for a short time, was a direct violation of existing Mexican law.

Dutton's resourcefulness could never by under-estimated. He recounted the tale of the limping yacht.

"Jay (McLaughlin) had an interest in a small airline in Palm Springs, and the chief pilot's name was Van Sickle. It was arranged for Van Sickle to pick up a complete engine kit, all the necessary tools, two qualified mechanics and fly them to the lonely little dirt airstrip at La Paz.

"Meanwhile, there was a taxi driver that I became acquainted with. He drove me back and forth to the dock when I went into the village for groceries and other errands.

"He had been a boxer and had been up to Montreal as a boy. He knew that I was a Canadian, and nobody else was going to drive a cab for me. When I wanted a car, I ran the Canadian flag up, and down to the dock he would come.

"We became good friends, and I was doing a good job of tipping him.

"I told him I was in trouble, so he came down to the boat where Jay and I explained what we wanted to do about bringing in Van Sickle and the mechanics.

"The cab driver told me to get mucho pesos, and we would have to talk to some policemen and customs officers.

"I gave this guy fifty pesos and that guy 100 pesos, and at seven o'clock that night, the little plane landed in La Paz and there wasn't a problem or a customs officer to be found anywhere.

"About a week later, when Van Sickle returned to pick up the mechanics and their tools, the officials impounded his plane.

"Then we had to start all over again, with the cab driver as a consultant. This time he suggested a nice party on the boat, with a lot of good Canadian meat and expensive booze.

"The cab driver brought four very official looking Mexicans down to the boat, and we put on the goddamnest spread you ever saw in your life. When they were leaving, we gave them each a bottle of champagne and a bottle of whiskey and they were happy as hell.

"I don't think anybody was ever more pleased to get out of Mexico than Van Sickle was, and as far as I know, he has never been back."

Reg and Merv enjoyed many diversions from the pressures of business. They both enjoyed hunting upland game birds and ducks and geese back in Alberta. Again, they combined their fondness with the sport with the corporation's public relations program, which had been conveniently designed to entertain existing and prospective clients.

One of the most prolific goose-hunting areas of North America is Sullivan Lake, a meandering, shallow alkali lake which stretches along a narrow draw about twenty-five miles south from Castor and Halkirk in east central Alberta.

Dutton and Jennings had befriended a local sportsman, Allan Mathias, the hardware store operator in Castor. When the ducks and geese were headed south in October and November, Mathias would telephone Reg and Merv in Calgary, and a shoot was quickly organized.

Characteristically, the partners were not satisfied to commute back and forth between Calgary and Castor, living in small-town hotels and eating in local cafes. Something much more elaborate was required. Something that would establish them on Sullivan Lake, and a place where they could eat and sleep in a manner which would meet their standards and a place where friends and clients could be royally entertained. It was an idea which had been perfected by European nobility since medieval times. A luxurious lodge in a private game preserve.

The first hurdle was to convince the provincial government that such an arrangement was worthwhile, and at the very least, did not discriminate against other residents of Alberta.

Permission was granted to build a lodge and an airstrip south of Halkirk on the north-east side of Sullivan Lake. Equipment, including ditchers and tractors were transported from Calgary to facilitate construction. Equipment was brought in to dig the pits used by the hunters as cover when the geese are flying. A comfortable, medium-sized lodge was erected, and vehicles were stored on the site that allowed the partners to commute between the lodge and Calgary in one of the company's small aircraft.

The Sullivan Lake Lodge became the site of many good times with Dutton and Jennings and friends.

Reg and Merv were both advocates of breeding and preservation programs for all game birds. Reg, for many years, was active in the Ducks Unlimited program that provided breeding and hatching grounds for ducks all over Western Canada. In his retirement, he devoted time and effort to fund-raising and other projects for Ducks Unlimited.

In 1965, the Upland Game Bird Association was formed with Merv Dutton as chief spokesman. The association was formed to ask the provincial government to pass legislation allowing game preserves in Alberta.

In a brief to government, the group argued that "free" bird hunting areas were becoming less and less accessible to the general public, and that private enterprise hunting preserves should be established where hunters would be charged a fee when they indulge their sport.

It said six Canadian provinces and forty-five states in the U.S. permit shooting preserves. Natural game bird populations are not disturbed. The operator buys eggs and chicks from hatcheries and raises them to adult age. He then releases them to be hunted on the preserve. The establishment of private game preserves was a long time in coming to Alberta; and a good part of the initial groundwork was laid by Reg and Merv. Both men remained in the field of game bird preservation well into their retirement years.

As the retirement years approached, the partners each bought a vacation home on the Borrego Springs Golf Course, an idyllic enclave tucked in a mountain valley south of Palm Springs, California. Each day away from winter included a game of golf, late afternoon relaxation around the pool patio in what Merv described as the "readjustment hour." He would pluck oranges from his tree, squeeze them to juice and serve his brand of screwdrivers. Then it was time to go out for dinner.

Dutton liked Chinese food. The Borrego Springs clubhouse boasted a fine Chinese chef and Dutton enjoyed the fare frequently. One evening Dutton was advised there was to be no more Chinese food. He singled out the chef, who told him the board of directors had ordered cessation of Chinese food items on the menu.

"To hell with them," he barked. "We'll set up our own Chinese restaurant."

And soon he and the chef were partners in an oriental eatery outside the compound.

Dutton & Jennings:
the Standard Saga
✤

Prominence and success breed envy and suspicion. The little guy gets a vicarious kick out of seeing the big guy exposed in public for alleged wrong doings and sharp practice.

Reg and Merv discovered they were vulnerable to the wrath of public opinion quite because of the growth of their business enterprises and their personal prominence.

It was back in 1959, when Judge J.S. Turcotte was commissioned to investigate improprieties at City Hall in Calgary and to determine whether anyone who had dealings with the city gained an improper advantage because of gifts or favors to city officials.

It has become a Calgary legend known as the "Thirteen Bags of Cement Caper."

"We were in a helluva mess," Merv recalls. "We didn't have any idea about doing work for the mayor up in Banff . . . and the first thing we know we're called in front of the Turcotte commission to testify.

"I knew Judge Turcotte for years. He was from Lethbridge and I used to kid him . . . he didn't know concrete from cement for Christ sake . . . and Reg and I are getting our dirty linen hung out in public . . . all the newspapers all over the country."

Reg, pondering the event with a wry smile, did his best to reconstruct the events leading up to the Turcotte enquiry.

"The way the thing started — Burns and Dutton were building a service station in Banff for the Imperial Oil Company and Don MacKay was building a house in Banff. We had a Burns and Dutton truck running back and forth between Banff and Calgary hauling supplies. It was a daily run and not unnaturally Don MacKay found out about it.

"Apparently he had thirteen sacks of cement he wanted hauled to Banff, so he contacted Burns and Dutton and requested the truck pick up the cement at the City of Calgary stores.

"Somebody down there spotted the truck, smelled a rat and somehow the story was leaked to the Calgary Herald, and they made a hell of a story out of it.

"I think the Herald had been waiting in the weeds a long time for MacKay to slip, and they nailed him good on this one. Unfortunately for all of us, the mayor had neglected to pay the city for the cement, and since the Burns and Dutton truck was seen hauling the cement to Banff to a house where a Burns and Dutton sub-contractor was doing work for the mayor, we were up to our ears in it," Reg said.

"And Reg and I never knew a goddamn thing about it," said Merv.

Publicity surrounding the incident triggered the Turcotte Commission which became a full-scale enquiry into affairs of Calgary's city hall.

In more than forty years of doing business with all levels of government, there was never a hint that either Reg or Merv had curried favor in any way with anyone in a position to award road-building or construction contracts.

Merv had only to refer in his memory to the stern admonitions of C.D. Howe, who had advised him that the allocations of government contracts was to be on a competitive, business-like basis and no foolishness would be tolerated.

But sometimes the bigness and the bureaucracy of corporate and government organizations allow the performance of business to take place beyond the view of top management.

Mayor MacKay was refurbishing a home he had purchased in Banff and had made arrangements with Burns & Dutton to have the stone and masonry contractor build a fireplace in his sprawling, mountainside retreat.

Judge Turcotte, in an effort to make the connection between the mayor and Burns & Dutton, asked Bob Burns why the mayor had not dealt directly with the sub-contractor who was performing the work.

Burns conjectured that the mayor had made his approach to someone in the Burns & Dutton organization, and without giving the matter very much thought, assigned the stone mason to proceed with the work at the mayor's.

As the testimony unfolded, it turned out the fireplace did not function properly and the mayor had refused to pay the $1,700 construction and installation charge. Meanwhile, the sub-contractor had been paid by Burns & Dutton, and now Burns, Dutton and Jennings had become sitting ducks for the Commission and the media.

It was not a very happy period for any of them. The investigation droned on for weeks and poked into the intricate details of every transaction between Dutton, Jennings and Burns and all of the various Standard General companies which had been doing contract work with the city over a period of years.

The testimony got particularly spicy when Commission counsel Bill McGillivray zeroed in on the exchange of gifts between officials at City Hall and the Standard General companies.

Reg openly testified that he and Merv had personally selected Christmas gifts for the mayor and other civic officials on behalf of their companies, including the Kelwood Corporation, one of the city's major residential housing developers.

The value of the gifts indicated that there wasn't enough involved to influence civic officials on the allocation of major contracts.

The gifts for 1955 totalled $640 in value.

Mayor MacKay received a $50 gift certificate and a silver tray and jug valued at $113; former Commissioner Ivor Strong received a $50 gift certificate and a candelabra valued at $125; Commissioner Thomas received a $50 gift certificate and a coffee wagon valued at $135; and Harry C. Walshaw, engineer in charge of city street and road construction, was sent a china set valued at $117.

Value of gifts sent during 1957 were set at $272.

Mayor MacKay received a candelabra valued at $68; Mr. Thomas received a chair valued at $159; and Mr. Walshaw was sent a traveling bag valued at $45.

Gifts sent during 1958 were valued at a total of $354.

Mayor MacKay received television tables valued at $37, and Italian figurines valued at $62; Mr. Thomas received a thermos set valued at $30, television tables valued at $37, and a silver tray valued at $98; and Mr. Walshaw received a silver tray valued at $90.

Additional testimony revealed that civic officials had presented gifts to Dutton and Jennings and several of the key figures in their firms. The reason: they had become close personal friends over many years of close association through business dealings, and it seemed appropriate to exchange gifts at Christmas. City Commissioner E.C. Thomas told the Commission that he had received gifts from officials of Dutton and Jennings firms over the years, and he considered them gifts from individuals and not from the companies.

When Judge Turcotte made public his report on the enquiry, Reg and Merv were completely vindicated. Mayor MacKay did not fare so well, and was rejected by the voters of Calgary.

Dutton & Jennings:
the Standard Saga
❋

Leaders in trade, commerce and industry are often too immersed in business affairs to be community leaders as well. Not Reg and Merv.

With their far-flung business interests, both men displayed a zealous interest in community affairs, and both possessed natural qualities of leadership that kept them constantly in the community limelight.

Dink Carroll, late Sports Editor of the Montreal Gazette, had a visit with Merv and Reg back in 1962, and wrote in his column a succinct characterization of the two westerners:

"Chinook Hits Montréal . . . Following in the wake of a chinook wind that swept through the sub-zero prairies recently, and produced an Indian Summer atmosphere, two outstanding Western Canadian sportsmen paused briefly in Ourtown yesterday . . . they were Mervyn "Red" Dutton, former N.H.L president-manager-coach-player, and his right-and-left-hand business colleague, Reg Jennings . . . they represent one of the most unusual sports-business combinations since Damon and Pythias . . . when not engaged in the operation of a widespread contracting empire, Dutton and Jennings are linked with hockey, curling, football, golf and Stampedes in their adopted Calgary . . . latest sports venture is a 36-lane bowling establishment for the Foothills Metropolis . . . it's one of the most up-to-date plants west of Winnipeg . . . it's dedicated to five-pin bowling, an alley sport invented by the late Tommy Regan of Toronto, and popular from Ontario to Vancouver, but never accepted in Montreal or eastwards . . . as usual, Dutton did most of the talking and little of the listening as he hedge-hopped through Canadian sport in general, Calgary in particular . . . Jennings is England born, Saskatchewan raised and Calgary adopted . . . if I can remember all the things Dutton said about Canadian sport during his one hour, trip-hammer conversation, I'll endeavour to produce it in an early issue . . . he made some interesting observations on Canadian pro-football and what he sees in the immediate future . . . Jennings simply listening . . . 'I have to,' he explained at parting. 'Dutton's ears aren't good so they used to be. I'll have to go over what you said, including the limericks.'"

Dutton's contribution to community life was directed to a large extent by his keen interest in sport and sports promotion. It was a natural follow-up to his long career as NHL player, coach, manager and league president. In Calgary he was, among other things, president of the Stampeder Football Club and president of the internationally renowned Calgary Exhibition and Stampede.

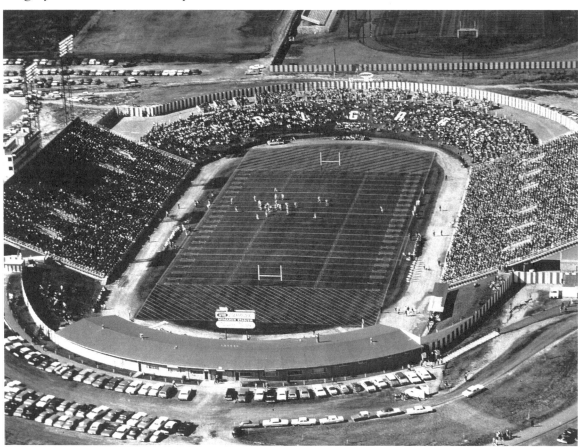

McMahon Stadium opening day, 1960 · *McMahon Stadium Society*

Not many men have displayed leadership qualities in as many different fields and locations as Merv Dutton. In the late 1950s, the Calgary Stampeders Football team had outgrown Mewata Stadium, its home field. Frank McMahon a pioneer oilman agreed to underwrite the cost of a new, much larger one. McMahon approached Dutton and Jennings with a proposition that included a fixed price and an almost impossible deadline. The job was completed on time, on budget in time for the 1960 season opener.

In the spring of 1941, Merv's name was featured on the marque of Madison Square Garden as the special feature guest at the Garden's annual dinner.

It was one of New York's important social events. The guests, including Mayor Fiorello La Guardia and legions of well-known personalities, needed no coaxing to attend.

At the dinner, Col. James Kilpatrick, President of Madison Square Garden, represented the feelings of most New Yorkers when he said: "No one person can take the credit for suggesting that you be the guest of honor at our Madison Square Garden dinner this year. It was a spontaneous outburst, and when word went around the grapevine that you were 'it', I wish you could have seen the enthusiasm of the gang.

"This annual party is a very special one – a family party of the Garden Gang – and while you yourself know full well that you are one of us, outsiders haven't always appreciated this fact, so here tonight is the answer!

"There are no halfway measures about our feelings towards you, Red. We hate you when you're battling our Rangers and we love you at other times, and I think, if we were completely honest, we would admit that we don't really even hate you at all, but admire you and think you're a swell guy all the time!"

Poems were written. New York columnists and sports writers chronicled his achievements in hockey and he had the unqualified respect of all NHL owners.

The feelings of everyone who knew him during fifteen tempestuous years in the NHL were best summarized by James Hurley of the New York Daily Mirror, and President of the New York Hockey Writers' Association.

"Those of us who have known Red Dutton since he entered the National Hockey League as a member of the Montreal Maroons in 1926 love him for his uncompromising frankness and the fiery combative spirit which helped to highlight one of the most interesting decades of major professional hockey.

"This never-say-die attitude of Merv Dutton is typical of the stock from which he comes, whose harried, war-encompassed natives in the mother country have earned the admiration of an astonished world by their ability to take it and to smile 'thumbs up' under the longest, fiercest air assault in the world's history.

"That same fighting nature enabled him to convalesce from a shell wound in World War I after 16 months in hospital to become one of the most rugged defensemen in big-time hockey. Murray Murdoch, one of the original Rangers, turned in a remarkable playing record when he participated in 600 consecutive games. But, Murray, an artful and hardy skater, didn't have to throw his weight into the foe as did Dutton, who with Shore, was one of the game's incredible iron men. We have seen Dutton playing game after game with various and assorted injuries ranging from a broken toe to cracked ribs, extensive charley horses and a broken wrist. Once as a member of the Maroons, he went 43 games without a relief.

"We hated Red Dutton as a member of the Maroons, through it was a compliment to his effectiveness in giving the works to our Rangers and Americans, but we soon came to love him for a fearless, honest athlete who gave everything in him for his team's cause every time he stepped out on the ice.

"Red never backed away from anything on a hockey rink, and as manager of the Americans, he has never refused to see a newspaper-man no matter how depressed by defeat or the affairs of his struggling club. He couldn't equivocate even to gain a place in seventh heaven, a trait that has made this volatile, impetuous pilot of the Americans universally beloved of hockey reporters."

When the Brooklyn Americans Hockey Club suspended operations at the end of the 1941-42 season, Dutton returned to Calgary to join Jennings in the contracting business.

That same summer, John Kilpatrick wanted him to become vice-president of hockey for the corporations, and Montreal Canadiens' president, Senator Donat Raymond, offered him the job as managing director of the hockey Canadiens. He rejected both offers, and the Montreal job was eventually filled by Frank Selke.

When Dutton was appointed full-time NHL president in 1945, he had the assurance of three governors: Senator Raymond, Major Frederic McLaughlin of Chicago, and James D. Morris of Detroit, that we would be awarded the Brooklyn franchise after the war, if he could get a rink built.

When the war had ended, and Red called on the governors to make good their promise, they welched. That incident lingers vividly in his memory, and well into his eighties, Merv's fiery temper surfaces when he recalls the story.

"It was the league's annual meeting in June, 1946 in New York. I had told them I was leaving the post of president because I wasn't being fair to Reg in the operation of the construction company. Clarence Campbell had been appointed president by the governors, and I had agreed to help him until he got settled in. Then I brought up the matter of the franchise in Brooklyn, which had been promised to me.

"Nobody said a damned word.

L–R: Merv Dutton & Lester Patrick in New York · *Hockey Hall of Fame*

"Finally, Connie Smythe says, 'Yes, Red, we've talked about that.'

"'What do you say about it?' I asked.

"'There are complications.'

"'What do you mean there are complications?'

"'Well for one thing, Madison Square Garden wants two franchises.'

"I couldn't believe it. I was mad! I told them I had backers in Brooklyn with a site and $7 million to build an arena."

"'Sorry Red, the Garden wants two franchises in New York!'

"I looked around that table and looked every one of those governors square in the eye. I told those governors where they could shove their franchise, and I walked out."

In 1951, Dutton was elected a director of the Calgary Exhibition and Stampede Board. Prior to that, he had some association with the Stampede through various construction projects. He had become a close personal friend of Maurice Hartnett, Stampede General Manager.

"Maurice and I were great friends and we spent lots of time around the grounds looking at improvements that should be done. Of course the money wasn't there as it is today; we had to watch our budget at all times and again, the crowds who paid the freight weren't as large as they are today."

The Stampede Board operated the professional Stampeder Hockey Club, which played in the Western Canada League and subsequently in the Pacific Coast Hockey League. Venerable Lloyd Turner was the manager, but Dutton maintained a watchful eye on player's salaries.

Sid Finney, one of the smoothest stick-handlers ever produced in Calgary, remembers Dutton as tough at the negotiating table and ever tougher as a critic of the team's performance on the ice.

"Gordon Love who was then head of the Board and was to be the next president of the Stampede Board," Dutton recalled. "He was invited to head up the Canadian Chamber of Commerce, and Gordon, being a great Commerce man, wanted this position very badly. He came to see me one Sunday night and said he was in trouble, that he would like to take the Chamber of Commerce job, but didn't want to lose his position in the Stampede. He felt that the directors would go along with his thinking that I could take over in his year, and he would follow me as president. I hadn't planned on this, but on the instigation of the directors, and after much discussion, I said I would do it. It was tough on me because I hadn't had the experience as a vice-president.

"I knew the inner workings of the Stampede, but with the help of the directors and all the staff, I felt that we had had a lot of bad weather, the price rise — that all in all, I had done a pretty fair job. I'd always felt that to be connected with the Stampede was an honor. It was an honor for me because I am not a native Calgarian. I was born in Winnipeg. The people that I had connections with are in my fondest of memories. Such fellows as Dick Cosgrave, Herman Linder, Duncan Renaldo (Cisco Kid), Leo Carrillo (Poncho), people like Bing Crosby, Bob Hope, all these people that are absolutely a legend with the Stampede.

"Others that participated in the Stampede were: the Burton Brothers, a couple of characters from Claresholm. Wilf Carter was another. What would the Stampede have been if it hadn't been for those kind of men? They were great participants, and they added so much to the Stampede.

"I recall John Diefenbaker opening our show in 1960. He had just been elected Prime Minister of Canada. It was quite a thing to have a Prime Minister, and it was well received by the patrons of the Stampede. Tragedy struck during a chuckwagon race in 1960; one of the drivers was killed. It was very sad. 1960 was memorable for its difficulties. We had trouble with the entertainment at the Corral when Roy Rogers and Dale Evans failed to appear, owing to Roy's illness. We contacted Johnny Cash who agreed to come but didn't. We had to do lots of improvising to keep the Corral in operation. In 1960, the gate charge was increased from twenty-five to fifty cents, and it was the year we instituted free attractions. It was the innovation of this part of the Stampede that has increased every year since. It was also the year of the Cisco Kid, Duncan Renaldo, who returned to Calgary. Duncan was a great attraction and a very fine man.

"It was also the year we put the cover over the East Grandstand. The new barns were built that year. You could see that Maurice's plans were starting to materialize. We started to put down pavement and asphalt. There were many anxious moments regarding finances, attendance and the general health of the Stampede. Much time was spent during the fall of 1960 and the spring of 1961, when we put the additional twenty-four sheets of ice in the Big Four Building, upper floor, making it the largest indoor curling rink in the world. It was highly publicized all over North America and was a great addition to the sports facilities in Calgary.

"1961 was a better year for us, as far as I was concerned. It was the year that we had Senora Eva DeLopes Mateos, wife of the President of Mexico. She was accompanied on her visit to the Stampede by her daughter and the Mexican Ambassador to Canada. They were very gracious and everyone loved them.

"1961 was the year of the inauguration of the Stampede Futurity for two-year-olds born in Canada. One of my great pleasures was that my partner, Reg Jennings, had won this prestigious race twice. The winning horses were Royal Attache and Alberta Blue. The thrills we had in racing were out of this world. The Stampede Futurity gets bigger and better every year. The purses are increased and the standard of horses has been much better. It's a great race, and it's a great chance for the breeders to show the quality of horses being raised in Western Canada.

"Many fine things happened to me or to the Stampede during 1961," Dutton said. "There were many things we had to improvise and take care of when we had no control over these events. One of these was the transit strike in Calgary. With the exception of opening day, all that week we were without transportation for the Stampede. In spite of this very troublesome thing, on the Friday we appealed to the citizens of Calgary to cooperate with us. An all-time attendance record up to that date of 36 875 was established on the Friday morning children show. People with cars gathered up kids who had no intention of going to the Stampede.

"This is the cooperation we had from the people of Calgary. The support we received from the people of Calgary was outstanding."

In June 1956, Calgary's new air terminal at McCall Field was opened. It was a Burns and Dutton job, so naturally Reg, Merv and Bob Burns were on hand for the opening ceremonies.

Mayor Don MacKay presided at the official opening.

"The work of building the new air terminal can certainly be appointed to with pride by this trio of Calgary men, and Reg Jennings, Red Dutton and Bob Burns will certainly be standing on the sidelines and watching with a sense of personal satisfaction, the tremendous amount of good will that the new air terminal building will generate for the City of Calgary," said the Mayor.

Reg was very active in the Shriner's organization, and had been appointed Honorary Lieutenant Colonel of the Royal Canadian Army Service Corps at Currie Barracks in Calgary. Reg was frequently called upon by civic, provincial and federal authorities to entertain dignitaries who visited Calgary.

In July 1959, the Queen and Prince Philip visited Calgary and the Stampede as part of a nation-wide Royal Tour. Reg and Beth Jennings were prominent among those who entertained the Royal Couple.

In the period language of the Herald's Women pages, a royal barbecue was described in intricate detail.

"Shortly before Her Majesty, the Queen, Prince Philip and the Royal Party arrived at the homes of Mr. Justice M.M. Porter and Mrs. Porter, and Mr. and Mrs. R.F. Jennings for the barbecue arranged in their honor, the sky clouded over and a chill wind blew in from the northeast.
"At 8 P.M., the sun hung low over the mountains and the scene atop the hill was breathtaking.
"Riders of the RCMP teepees dotted the valley below the spacious homes."

One of the most prestigious honors bestowed on Reg, was his appointment, in late 1960, to a directorship on the Toronto-Dominion Bank Board of Directors. It was rare for the barons of Bay Street to acknowledge business and financial acumen west of Toronto.

Reg's business career began as a bank clerk in Foremost back in 1922, and he enjoyed the irony of becoming bank director through a circuitous and arduous route of backbreaking toil as construction worker.

Reg's mail was flooded with congratulatory letters following the appointment. Typical was one from his friend Doug Dundas, President of the Great Falls National Bank.

Dear Reg:

I have a note on my desk from Jay (McLaughlin) in which he advises me that you are to be elected a director of the Toronto-Dominion Bank and are probably back there at this time to accept.

This is a very fine recognition for you, Reg, and one that is sought by many men, I am sure. Because of the comparatively few banks in Canada and the widespread branch system there, bank directorships are not plentiful and in that respect are quite different from those in the United States. So I feel it is a real honor to you and I am most happy to see you get it. I am sure you will find your association most interesting and enjoyable, and I wish for you the very best of success.

We have neglected to open an account with any Canadian bank partly due to the fact there does not seem to be as much need for it today as there was a couple of years ago. But I can assure you with the recognition you have now received from the Toronto-Dominion Bank we may hasten our decision and, of course, it cannot be any other bank than the one of which you are a director.

With kindest personal regards to you and Beth, I am

Sincerely,
Doug Dundas
President

Reg had won the respect of all segments of the community, and through his generosity and concern, became a close friend of Southern Alberta's Indians. Reg encouraged them in their arts and crafts and was a substantial patron of these endeavors.

As part of their Centennial year celebrations in 1967, the Blood Indians of Cardston staged a large-scale rodeo and week of celebrations at Standoff, Alberta. A feature of the celebration was induction of five prominent Canadians, including Reg Jennings as Honorary Chief of the tribe. Reg was dubbed Chief Red Tailfeathers.

The ceremony, which attracted more than 2,000 spectators, many of them in traditional Indian dress, was part of a celebration which included eighteen tribes from U.S. and Canada, a rodeo, track and field events, dancing and a costume parade.

The induction ceremony was an intriguing spectacle conducted by five medicine men who dance to the beat of a drum, paint their visions on those being inducted into the tribe, and finally place a headdress on the Honorary Blood Indian and give him his new title.

Reg was a strong believer of preserving the heritage of Alberta, and put his weight and money behind several restoration projects. He was a prime mover in Calgary's Heritage Park project. He was particularly keen about the history of Southern Alberta in the Lethbridge-Fort Macleod area.

Reg, Beth and Harold Millican journeyed to Fort Macleod on an early June Saturday in 1980 to participate in ceremonies commemorating the life of pioneer lawyer and politician Sir Frederick W.G. Haultain.

Reg had financed the restoration of Haultain's law office on the Fort Macleod site. Millican was the principal speaker of the day and reviewed the highlights of Haultain's life. Fort Macleod Mayor Ken Hurlburt presented Reg with an original oil painting by Blood Indian artist Gerald Tailfeathers for his gift to the museum. He acknowledged Reg's many gifts to Fort Macleod, including the swimming pool and the tennis court.

Al Scarth, of The Lethbridge Herald, captured both the significance of the event and Reg's light-hearted mood in his coverage of the Haultain memorial.

"A Calgary construction magnate who partnered in bedecking the province with airports, crisscrossing it with its first paved highways and straddling it with the Trans-Mountain pipeline, will open his latest project in Fort Macleod Saturday — an old log building.

"It will be 46 years since Reg Jennings first entered the Fort for the Golden Jubilee of the Northwest Mounted Police. In fact, Reg Jennings' arrivals there always seem to mark some historic occasion.

"In 1926 he returned to produce the gravel for the first graveled road between the Fort and Calgary. After that his companies partnered with Red Dutton and built the first roads across the Indian reserves and generally sewed the district up with paved highways.

"That old log building he is coddling ('Mind you, I haven't seen it since its completion') is a monument to another and different kind of pioneer.

"The original law office of Sir Frederick Haultain-one-time premier of the Northwest Territories, Chief Justice of the Saskatchewan Supreme Court and probably the foremost pioneer behind educational reform in the fledging provinces of Alberta and Saskatchewan-now stands its original site in restored condition.

"That's Reg Jennings' latest project. Now semi-retired at 67, the company timekeeper who ended up owning several giant construction firms, explains: 'The people of Fort Macleod have been very kind to me and I suggested a couple of years ago that I would be interested in contributing something to the Fort Macleod Historical Association.'

"The association subsequently asked Mr. Jennings to help restore the original office of the Fort's illustrious political and educational reformer, as a lasting contribution to the district.

"Now, two years later, it stands on a site attached to the Fort Macleod Museum, 'right where it was built about 1885.'

"While Alberta's 'oldest living paving contractor' no longer has his own office in the town he helped join to the rest of the province, he has restored not only a landmark, but a sentimental link with an area which gave him one of his first starts.

"A director of several firms, Mr. Jennings also sits as chairman of the board for Standard General Construction International Ltd. He has disposed of most of his interests in the companies created over the last 35 years in partnership with

Hockey Hall of Fame star Red Dutton, retaining only the management of Calgary's sprawling Chinook Shopping Centre in conjunction with his son Roy.

"One informal supervisory position he has taken care to maintain: that of keeping a close watch over Calgary's Heritage Park. This extensive landmark is in full view from the Jennings' sixth floor spacious apartment in nearby Eagle Ridge.

"The park itself may soon be a personal link with the past for Mr. Jennings and his son, Roy, Executive Vice-President of Chinook. Roy Jennings hopes to relocate a certain set of barber chairs to the park. They belonged to his grandfather.

"My father was quite a roamer," chuckles the senior and also well-traveled Jennings: "From southern Saskatchewan to southern Alberta to northern Alberta. He did a little bit of everything. He was a barber by trade, but along with the shop he ran a billiard hall and bowling alley."

"The Jennings hope to bring the chairs, now in Foremost, to the Barons Billiard Hall which has been relocated to the park and in which partners Jennings and Dutton are scheduled to hit the first relocated cue ball when it opens.

"There is one other nostalgic event Reg Jennings isn't likely to miss. He made it to the Golden Jubilee of the famous mounted predecessors to the RCMP and his own fiftieth anniversary with Fort Macleod's 100th is only four years away."

Reg and Merv both had a keen awareness of where their wealth originated, and both were spontaneous in their conviction that "casting bread upon the water" is good citizenship as well as good business.

When Standard Gravel was at the peak of its early growth period in 1952, Reg and Merv had decided on a commemorative gesture to honor the memory of their respective fathers. They decided on a cancer therapy unit as a gift to the people of Alberta.

Alberta Premier Ernest Manning acknowledged the gesture in a letter to Reg on December 30, 1952.

I have before me your letter advising that it is the wish of yourself and Mr. Mervyn A. Dutton to present to the people of Alberta a cobalt therapy machine in memory of Mr. Horace John Jennings and Mr. William A. Dutton, the said machine to be used in the Provincial Cancer Clinic for the treatment of those suffering from cancer. On behalf of the government and the people of Alberta, I gratefully accept your generous offer and thank you most sincerely for your kindness. Your thoughtful and generous act, I know, will be appreciated deeply by every citizen of this province, who I am sure, will agree that you could have not chosen a more fitting memorial to the memory of your late father nor one that will do more to alleviate the anxiety and suffering of those afflicted by cancer.

Again, on behalf of the government, the citizens of Alberta and those who will be helped individually as a result of your kind and thoughtful act, may I express grateful thanks and sincere appreciation.

Yours very truly,
"Ernest Manning"
Premier

The therapy unit, delivered to the clinic in Edmonton in 1953, was widely acclaimed as "new hope for cancer sufferers in Alberta".

It was manufactured by the commercial products division of Atomic Energy of Canada Limited. The radio-active isotope which served as the source of radiation was a product of the Canadian government's atomic pile at Chalk River, Ontario.

The unit was installed in a special therapy room with forty-four inches of concrete shielding on the wall in front of the unit, and concrete side walls of twenty-two-inch thickness, tapering to twelve-inch thickness.

Reg and Merv knew where their money came from: hard work and opportunities provided by the growth of Western Canada. They were always prepared to put some back in for a worthwhile cause. Well into their retirement years, both men continued to support a long list of fraternal and community organizations. Prior to the formation of the Alberta Roadbuilders' Association, Merv Dutton served a term as president of the Prairie Roadbuilders Association. In a tribute to the founders of Standard-General, the Alberta Roadbuilders Association conferred Honorary Life Memberships on Reg Jennings and Merv Dutton at the annual convention in 1981.

Reg's son Roy who continued his involvement in the management of the Chinook Shopping Centre backed up his father's community service, even to the extent of serving a stint as president of the Calgary Stampeders football team. Reg died in 1982.

Merv Dutton served the community long into retirement. Prominent among his projects was his support of the Springbank Community Association and the Red Dutton Arena. He died March 15, 1987.

Dutton & Jennings:
the Standard Saga

*

JOHN DENHOLM later compiled a chronology of the company's evolution and future affiliations. "I remember after the sale to the employees wondering why we could never get our hands on the dividends. The company was thriving and profitable. We had to get used to the idea that the profits were directed to Reg and Merv until the sales agreement with employees was paid out."

"As I figure it," recalled John, "S-G (Standard Gravel) during my association, had about ten or eleven stages in its management or ownership history."

In the beginning, Standard Gravel & Surfacing Co. Ltd. was formed April 10, 1941 with $9 paid in capital, with Merv and Reg each having two shares each, and one share each held by Jack Dutton, Fred Owens, Bob Paget, Ken Paget and Murray Dodds.

Sometime during 1944, Merv and Reg bought out the other five shareholders, to own and manage 100% of Standard Gravel and Surfacing.

During the 1950s, a new company, Standard Gravel & Surfacing of Canada Ltd. was formed with employee shareholders, to buy out SGS from Dutton & Jennings.

In 1960, SGS Management Limited was formed to buy out the smaller employee shareholders in SGS of Canada. Standard Holdings Limited was formed to provide overall management of Dutton and Jennings interests, owned by a small group of employees, including a management group of S-G. Standard bought General Construction of Vancouver, broadening its operating management group, and changed its name to Standard-General Construction Ltd. Following the sale to the employees, Standard Gravel began a journey of many incarnations and owners.

In 1968, Standard Holdings Ltd., its subsidiary Standard-General and other smaller interests including Consolidated Concrete and others was sold to BACM Industries of Winnipeg. Majority control of BACM in turn was acquired by Sogemines Ltd. of Montreal, a subsidiary of Societe Generale de Belgique of Belgium. Sogemines' name was changed to Genstar Corporation. Management of the Standard Group was assumed by the Simkin family of Winnipeg, former owners of BACM.

"I knew and respected Saul Simkin," recalled John Denholm. "He was a big picture person who didn't interfere as long as the company performed and the profits rolled in. His son

'Blackie' on the other was more of a hands on, micro manager to the annoyance of many of the employees."

In 1976, the Simkin family group retired, the BACM name disappeared and management of Genstar's construction, materials, and pre-cast operations in Canada and the United States was assumed by Len Holman, an Executive V-P of Genstar.

Standard Gravel & Surfacing reunion party, 1964

In 1986, Genstar Corporation was taken over by Imasco Ltd. and most divisions other than financial services were sold off. Cement, construction, materials and precast divisions were sold by Imasco to CBR Cement, an affiliate of SGB, the Belgian-based original founders of Genstar. CBR continued its corporate office in Calgary for Canada, with main management controlled from U.S. corporate headquarters in San Mateo, CA. Over the next few years, CBR sold precast and some materials operations to management groups, concentrating on cement, concrete and aggregates, but retaining the construction divisions, Standard-General, in Alberta.

About 1990, Societe Generale de Belgique, parent of CBR Cement was attacked by Italian take-over artist, Carlos de Benedetti. Rather than be taken over by an Italian group "the nouveau riche of Europe", SGB accepted an offer from another French-speaking group, Groupe Suez, of Paris, which demonstrated little change in operating style.

Denholm recalled that in 1994, Groupe Suez ran into tough times, mainly with its banking operations, and sold CBR Cement to Heidelberg Cement Co. of Heidelberg, Germany. Heidelberg already had North American operations as Lehigh Portland Cement Co., headquartered in Allentown, Pennsylvania.

Lehigh launched a strategy to close corporate offices in Calgary and San Mateo, and transferred some key people to Allentown. Operations were organized on a regional basis, with prairie operations run by the cement company operating in the area, Inland Cement of Edmonton.

In June 1996, Inland contemplated discontinuing the trade names Standard-General and Consolidated, and to operate the companies under Inland Construction, and Inland Aggregates names. It didn't follow through and the original company names prevailed.

In John Denholm's opinion the name change idea was scrapped because somebody reminded the owners that Genstar toyed with this idea in the early 1970s, but was headed off by the Simkin family. "Blackie and Saul knew the value of the S-G and Consolidated names in Alberta."

Terry Gale, current Vice-President and General Manager of Standard-General Inc, has been with the company for thirty years. His career began as an estimator.

"In the beginning I didn't pay much attention to corporate ownership. When they eventually gave me a half-ton truck and a crew to undertake projects I was happy."

Terry Gale

Gale departed the company for two years largely due to philosophical differences in operating objectives. Upon his return in June of 2002, Gale was appointed vice-president for the Calgary operations of Standard General Inc. In April 2007, the company opened its' new Calgary Operations Centre, containing a very modern facility designed to house an office, maintenance facility, equipment storage yard and asphalt plant.

Standard General is currently owned by COLAS, a large multi-national Civil Construction company. The name COLAS is a contraction of cold asphalt a by-product of oil refineries originally marketed by Shell Oil in Europe.

From the beginning, the Standard Gravel office and yard was located off the Macleod Trail in the Manchester industrial district. As the twenty first century dawned, Calgary and Western Canada generally promised unprecedented growth in the economy and infrastructure construction requirements. In contemplation of this, Standard was restructured with autonomous branches in Calgary and Edmonton. Under Terry Gale's guidance, plans were developed for an expansion of Standard's plant and buildings at a new twenty-three acre site located in the newly developed Shepard Business Park in southeast Calgary. The new complex includes a 16,000 square foot, two storey office building, four acre equipment storage yard, 30,000 square foot modern equipment repair depot and fifteen acres designated for the new state of the art, environmentally sensitive asphalt plant complete with recycling capabilities.

Standard's new office & asphalt plant in southeast Calgary, 2008 · *Darren Colton*

Bill Gardiner, a retired official with Standard's operation in Edmonton, described the company's history in the northern city.

In the fall of 1969, Standard General opened offices in Edmonton under the direction of Arnold Berg. Arnold assembled a group of key people, mostly from the Calgary operations in order to establish a fully independent division in Edmonton. The main purpose of establishing in Edmonton was to service land being assembled by BACM Development (Genstar) in the metropolitan area. It would require Standard to enter into the sewer and water underground utilities business, a construction field new to Standard General.

The Edmonton group met the challenge on an all-out schedule to bring together the various elements, including personnel and equipment to organize all phases of the construction operation. Operations included: sewer and water installation; dirt moving and grading; sidewalks, curbs and gutters; soil cement mixing and installation; dry aggregate pit with crushing equipment and an asphalt plant and asphalt installation.

In the spring of 1979 Standard was the successful bidder for a large subdivision development for Home Smith Properties in Sherwood Park. This was the first of many projects performed for Home Smith over the years.

In 1971 Genstar launched its first subdivision in the Castle Downs area. Since this was a new area to be developed, it involved major trunk lines for sewer and water as well as major construction of arterial roadways.

Standard General went on to become one of the largest subdivision contractors in the Edmonton region and the only contractor to offer a complete package for subdivision development including the construction of many arterial and major roadway projects.

Mr. Gardiner said Standard's well earned reputation as one of the most respected and reliable contractors in the Edmonton area is due mainly to the dedication and hard work of its employees over the years.

The Standard-General bright orange and yellow logo can be seen on a wide variety of construction projects around Calgary and Edmonton. The company focuses on sewer and water, sidewalks curb and gutter, base preparation and asphalt paving in conjunction with the project management of large infrastructure projects in the greater Calgary area, it recently completed a twenty-two million dollar share of the major overpass and interchange at Glenmore Trail and Elbow Drive in south Calgary.

Acknowledgements

*

THE ENTHUSIASM AND COOPERATION of Reg Jennings and his longtime partner Mervyn (Red) Dutton made it possible to record this important chapter in Canada's industrial and construction history. For days on end in their Calgary office and at their homes in Southern California, Reg and Merv submitted to relentless taped interviews that covered their biographical and business histories. Roy Jennings, son of Reg, was instrumental in promoting the project.

After lying dormant for several years, the manuscript gathered dust until it was resurrected by the author with the encouragement of Gerry Stotts, P.Eng., who felt it provided important information to add to his efforts of preserving roadbuilding and construction history in Canada. Terry Gale, current Vice President and General Manager of Standard General Inc., agreed. Several former employees, including John Denholm, Keith Matthews, Jim McHendry, Arnold Welter also cooperated with their observations and comments. Pamela Gorman's contribution in computer services, research, and chasing down photos — along with Donna Maier, Office Administrator — were invaluable, as was Lois Mooney, with her expertise in photo reproduction. And also to James Dangerous of Detselig Enterprises for his invaluable assistance in his design, layout and editing.

In the search for pictures, valuable assistance was received from Bill Hay, Chairman of the Hockey Hall of Fame; Daryl Birnie of the McMahon Stadium Society; Gary Baird, Operations Manager of the Boundary Dam, Washington State; Arnold Welter; Roy Jennings; and the Glenbow Foundation.

Jᴏʜɴ T. "Jᴀᴄᴋ" Gᴏʀᴍᴀɴ, born in Alberta, educated at Notre Dame College, Saskatchewan, the University of Ottawa, was awarded certificate of proficiency from Columbia University seminar for editorial writers. His career included several years on editorial staff assignments at the Calgary Herald and Vancouver Sun; Public Relations Director of  the Canadian Petroleum Association, and together with his wife Pamela, published several rural newspapers. He is the author of six books and dozens of magazine articles.